IVP *Crescendo*

COURAGE. CONFIDENCE. CALLING.

Some voices challenge us. Others support or encourage us. Voices can move us to change our minds, draw close to God, discover a new spiritual gift. The voices of others are shaping who we are.

The voices behind IVP Crescendo join together to draw us into God's story. We'll discover God's work around the globe even as we learn to love the people around the corner. We'll have opportunity to heal our places of pain. We'll discover new ways to love our families. We'll hear God's voice speaking into our lives as we discover new places of influence.

IVP Crescendo invites you to join in the rising chorus

- *to listen to the voices of others*
- *to hear the voice of God*
- *and to grow your own voice in*

COURAGE. CONFIDENCE. CALLING.

ivpress.com/crescendo
ivpress.com/crescendo-social

Luci Shaw

# ADVENTURE
# *of* ASCENT

*Field Notes from a Lifelong Journey*

≋
IVP Books

An imprint of InterVarsity Press
Downers Grove, Illinois

*InterVarsity Press*
*P.O. Box 1400, Downers Grove, IL 60515-1426*
*World Wide Web: www.ivpress.com*
*Email: email@ivpress.com*

*InterVarsity Press® is the book-publishing division of InterVarsity Christian Fellowship/USA®, a movement of students and faculty active on campus at hundreds of universities, colleges and schools of nursing in the United States of America, and a member movement of the International Fellowship of Evangelical Students. For information about local and regional activities, write Public Relations Dept., InterVarsity Christian Fellowship/USA, 6400 Schroeder Rd., P.O. Box 7895, Madison, WI 53707-7895, or visit the IVCF website at www.intervarsity.org.*

*Scripture quotations, unless otherwise noted, are from the New Revised Standard Version of the Bible, copyright 1989 by the Division of Christian Education of the National Council of the Churches of Christ in the USA. Used by permission. All rights reserved.*

*While all stories in this book are true, some names and identifying information in this book have been changed to protect the privacy of the individuals involved.*

*Cover design: Cindy Kiple*
*Interior design: Beth Hagenberg*
*Image: Cut Bank-Sea Landscape by Clare Froy, UCL Art Museum, University College London*

*ISBN 978-0-8308-4310-7 (print)*
*ISBN 978-0-8308-7188-9 (digital)*

*Printed in the United States of America* ∞

**Library of Congress Cataloging-in-Publication Data**
*A catalog record for this book is available from the Library of Congress.*

| P | 17 | 16 | 15 | 14 | 13 | 12 | 11 | 10 | 9 | 8 | 7 | 6 | 5 | 4 | 3 | 2 | 1 |
|---|----|----|----|----|----|----|----|----|---|---|---|---|---|---|---|---|---|
| Y | 28 | 27 | 26 | 25 | 24 | 23 | 22 | 21 | 20 | 19 | 18 | 17 | 16 | 15 | 14 | | |

*Dedicated to those who have already summited*

# Contents

# Acknowledgments

*That this book,* born and reborn multiple times with different intentions and formats, has finally reached publication seems quite miraculous to me. Originally it was written to cover the seasons of the calendar year and the church year; later it was torn apart to reflect a metaphor—the stages of aging viewed as a mountain-climbing expedition. Writing the book became an adventure in itself!

Along the way I owe more than I can adequately say in gratitude for helpers more far-sighted than I, who was no longer able to look objectively at what I had written. Mary Kenagy Mitchell read an early draft of the book and gave me many insightful comments. Lauren Winner read it through in one evening and sent me a blurb on the spot. Lil Copan deserves the highest plaudits, clarifying, refocusing, slogging along with me through the text to make the book hold together. Patience, loving perseverance and skill are her other names, and I love her for how she helped this book to evolve and kept me from gloom and blockage. My brilliant agent Kathy Helmers took me on enthusiastically when Lee Hough, my other gifted literary agent, had to bow out due to grave illness. Lee had responded with such enthusiasm to the idea of the book. Later Kathy's wide experience and thoroughness brought the project to the attention of Cindy Bunch at

InterVarsity Press, where I feel like a member of a family. I've known Cindy's professionalism and enthusiasm over the years and feel secure in her hands. Gratitude as well to Ruth Goring for her perceptive and thorough reading and copyediting.

At an early stage I read parts of the manuscript to a couple of church groups. I also fed it in bits to members of the Chrysostom Society. I got such great feedback from these other women and men about my accounts of getting older, with its challenges and opportunities, that I was encouraged to keep writing.

Profound thanks also to my family tribe for sustaining me through this labor, encouraging the book to be born and grow. They are all part of the story—Robin, Marian, John, Jeffrey and Kristin. My husband, John, ever an optimistic and encouraging presence, has hovered in the background of everything I do; I could not have finished this book without him.

# A Word to My Readers

*The climb of my life* offered to you in this story has been both arduous and thrilling. As I've hiked this long slope of living, there have been crevasses to avoid or scramble out of, and mountain paths that wind high and low through immense evergreen forests. I've stumbled often, have fallen, been bruised and abraded. I've had to avoid sharp rock outcroppings and endured earth tremors as well as being awestruck by magnificent views of heaven and earth.

I remember how, from a mountain peak, Moses' mind was marked with a vision of the Promised Land for his wilderness-wandering people. And how though he never entered it for himself, he gave them hope for their future. I have no certain vision for the future beyond desires and longings; I have some regrets but also great gratefulness. I can look back and see how my trajectory flung a banner across the foothills.

I often wish that my life had unspooled neatly inch by inch across this varied landscape, like a thread that can be examined for flaws and tangles and shrinkage as it unwinds. But since it cannot be rewound, I have to rely on memory and experience and physical evidence—photos and journal entries and letters—to tell you some of what these recent years are like.

I want to describe to you my journey, in what ways it is

unique, just as yours is. I want to convey to you how morning and evening light differ, how the lungs and leg muscles ache as they climb, searching for footholds, often resting to take in the view over a pleat of the gradient.

I want to describe how good it is, sometimes, to simply let grass grow under my feet or feel the sun rest on my shoulder blades, or to pick a few berries from the bushes, or to watch the sun rise and set and rise again.

It has been, it *is*, a great adventure, this expedition we call human existence, though it is not always one that we might have chosen. It's a partnership, really, between the One who gives each of us life to start with and what we do with that incomparable gift.

Often, shadows like storm clouds have shielded the sun, or a thick mist has disoriented me. Snow squalls and a biting wind often pick up, and then I huddle with other climbers, refugees in small shelters like mountaineers in alpine huts during a blizzard.

Just as the sun is often hidden behind clouds, God's face has often seemed to be obscured, and then, when I feel most alone in my human frailty, I feel abandoned and vulnerable. I've learned a lot about waiting, and longing, for the light to return, for travel fatigue to fade as energy seeps into my bones again.

I plan to tell you about my frequent need to stop and check and find my bearings again, as if with a spiritual GPS. I surmise that there are no straight lines to the top, no mile markers to tell me when I might summit this mountain. When the peak is outlined cleanly against a glowing sky it looks attainable, even welcoming, but I know that such views can be deceptive; it may be a false summit with the real one much farther away than I can see. Warning signs about avalanches or steep declivities show up and cause anxiety for all of us on this trek.

This is a story with many stops and starts. Some questions

with no immediate answers. Doubts that weigh heavily and are not easily resolved. Many admissions of failure. High hopes and purposes as well as detours and uncertainties. And triumphs and revelations that sometimes overwhelm my astonished soul.

Yes, this has been a magnificent adventure. I invite you to come and view it with me!

# 1

# The View from Here

*I see us wherever I go.* The ones who are old enough to be full of the accumulated wisdom and insight of a rich lifetime. The ones whose faces still betray a certain confidence and fortitude. The ones who continue to have optimism about the future of the human race, and hope still to contribute to it. And the ones who have gone blank; who are saying to themselves, *What's the use?* (Though that's not a question; it's more a statement of reality.) These are the ones who don't have the energy to care anymore. It makes me wonder: is there a difference between acceptance (*It is what it is. Live with it*) and passivity (*I just can't be bothered anymore*)?

We are an aging population, and we crowd the malls and the churches and the supermarkets and airports and streets. We look for elevators instead of stairways. We get around in wheelchairs, or scooter chairs, or the special carts the supermarkets provide for the disabled (after surgery I've used them, and they work well enough, allowing some mobility for the ordinaries of living). If we can still pass our driving test and take to the road, we drive a bit more cautiously and hang our blue-and-white handicapped placard from our rearview mirror to claim the reserved spaces in the parking lot. There seem to be more and more such spaces allotted for our use. For them, too, I am grateful.

I've learned to take my placard with me when I travel, so that if I rent a car in some other city I can use it. I watch for those special parking spots with their blue-and-white signs. They mean that I won't have to walk so far to get to some entrance, some destination.

We are bent and slow, and our gait is often constricted by pain. We get the AARP bulletin in the mail that gives us advice about how to perk up our sex life and deal with the social security crisis. Though demographics show that we are achieving political power, weakness, slowness and caution have begun to characterize our movements. We plod. You could call our speed deliberate, because we almost have to *deliberate* before mounting the next step. Some of us are accompanied on our grocery outings—perhaps a younger woman, a graying spouse, an equally frail friend, or just our own cane as a companion.

Our expressions vary; some have a grin for anyone who greets them; some project enthusiasm and optimism; some faces are drawn with effort and ache. The expressions of some seem to define what loneliness looks like. A kind of interior resignation etches many features. From the language of the body I translate it as *What else can I do?* We keep going. It's our only option.

*Like the smoke that pollutes the sky somewhere*
*I'm a dream that dissolves in endless air.*
*So why should I care that I'm losing my hair?*

When I see this kind of shriveling in another human being, I automatically straighten up, walk taller and try to pull in my stomach. It's a sign to myself that I haven't given up yet. My mother had a thing about good posture, and I was well-trained, made to walk around the house balancing a book on my head, which requires a truly vertical spine. Mother lived to ninety-nine, though against her iron will arthritis eventually curled her into a human comma.

I used to be proud of myself that I could run up and down a flight of stairs. My father raced, *two steps* at a time, up any staircase he encountered around the world until he was over eighty. Perhaps for both of us it was a kind of showing off, a bravado, a way of defying the odds, of proving that disability hadn't caught up with us. Yet. I'm still in a house with stairs. I take a nap in the afternoon. My study is on the ground floor, but having our bedroom upstairs means I must make several climbs a day to the second floor. I tell myself it keeps me mobile.

It hurts a lot, especially my left knee, which has only recently been "replaced" like its right counterpart. It doesn't want to bend much, so it hurts even more coming down the stairs, even though gravity is on my side. Tylenol for Arthritis is my constant friend.

But it was Emerson who said: "People do not *grow* old. When they cease to grow they *become* old."

So there's a goal I'm aiming for. To keep growing, even as the number of years add up, and up. And in this book I hope to act as a scout moving into new territory and reporting back to the coming generation so that you may know what it's like, and what to be ready for.

### The Door, the Window

*To get older is to watch the door close inch by inch*
*against my will so that the inflow of silky air*
*stops, and the creek's subtleties of sound.*
*In the small house of my ear I listen closely to*
*the message of blood, knowing others are deaf to it,*
*as I begin to be to their soft speech across*
*the dinner table. My memory thins; names drift*
*just beyond the rim of recollection. I'm told*
*the floaters in my right eye are only gel thickening*
*into dark splinters that diminish the light.*

*"Nothing can be done," my doctor says. "You'll*
*get used to them." I am not getting used to them.*
*My years undermine me, eating away in the dark,*
*silent as carpenter ants in the beams. The pine mirror*
*in the bathroom reflects my white slackness; why*
*are my cells failing me just when I am*
*getting the hang of their glistening life? The minutes*
*wear me away—a transparent bar of glycerin soap,*
*a curved amber lozenge dissolving*
*in daily basins of water. The window glass, brittle*
*as the scalloped collars of ice that shrink our stream,*
*still opens its icon eye to me, allows me to see*
*across the sun-struck grass, white with frost, to hear*
*the water telling its winter story, telling mine.*[1]

Then I remember the tale of Bilbo Baggins: "'Go back?' he
thought. 'No good at all! Go sideways? Impossible! Go forward?
Only thing to do! On we go!'"

～

At the outset I must let you know my purpose for this
chronicle. I plan to document my life as it moves toward the
summit. I don't know what lies ahead, but I'm committing
myself to noting things that seem worthwhile or significant. To
report on reflections, insights, new news and old news, in the
hope that I may shed a clean light on what it's like to be edging,
inevitably, toward . . . ?

This onward movement is inexorable. Almost every week
now I get news of colleagues and contemporaries who have left
us. I'm getting used to the word *die* and would rather use it than
the euphemisms "give up the ghost," "pass away," "pass on" or
simply "pass." *Deceased* is a terribly technical word for me—

impersonal, what a coroner might say about a body discovered after an accident. Some Christians talk about their family members "going home," but I wonder if the strange new atmosphere of heaven will feel homelike. Dying is an unshrinking reality that can't be euphemized with any authenticity except by those who are already dead and who, because the lines of communication have been severed, cannot tell us what it was like. I want to cut to the bone about this business of being old and getting older. So you'll know and understand. So you'll know and not fear.

In this telling I vow to be scrupulously honest about myself and the events in my life. I will not fudge about my flaws or attainments. I will try to be compassionate about the failings of others and celebrate their triumphs.

If aging is a disease, its name is senescence. There's a well-developed branch of medicine to deal with it, gerontology. It's all well and good to name this condition and refer to it in textbooks. Living it, living with it, gives it a face and an array of recognizable symptoms.

The trouble with aging is that there's really no remedy. In the end, no one survives it.

Unless they themselves have some kind of fatal disease, young people rarely feel the threat of death or diminishment. They expect to keep going forever. For youth, the fires of energy flow through them and feel inextinguishable. Young people expect to climb the mountains of possibility with a vitality that slowly begins to ebb, I'm told, in their thirties, though when I was thirty such a thought hadn't entered my mind (I was too busy with four children and a new business to run with my husband). In early adulthood I was, as Sarah Payne Stuart describes it, "still radiant with the delusions that brighten the threshold of middle age."[2] Gradually it becomes apparent to all of us that eternal youth is a myth, except for minds alive to possibility, or perhaps fantasy.

Of course, for authenticity, I'm writing as a woman. But my male counterparts may be asking similar questions, searching for meaning as I do. They also experience comparable physical deterioration, with some minimal differences. They may have prostate problems or erectile dysfunction, and they tend to lose more hair, while I am liable to pee from sudden sneezing or laughing too hard (I do a lot of laughing and I have an overdeveloped sense of irony), and I worry about osteoporosis. A recent bone-density test revealed that I have ostopoenia, a dwindling of bone mass, though I've taken calcium and vitamin D3 scrupulously for years.

Both genders dread the loss of independence and the onset of dementia, conditions that loom like the sickle of the black-robed Grim Reaper over our purposes and plans. I recently learned of a brilliant friend's bereavement after her husband's death from stroke. She is a good bit younger than I and she has dementia, and now, without a family caregiver, she must join the ranks of others in a home for Alzheimer's patients. It is grievous to see what can happen to such a vigorous human mind.

Jeanne Walker sent me a new poem today. Her unique singing voice comes through so clearly. She picks up on details but pulls them together with other seemingly unrelated details to form a new dynamic whole. One image she used described her "fiasco" of a lawn, and the daffodils that "clamber up like miners / still bravely shining their yellow headlamps." I wrote back to her about that description—how I loved it—but in my letter I typed in "dandelions" instead of "daffodils." I guess the color golden yellow was what had stayed with me, and my mind did the floral transposition unawares, until I saw it later and wondered if this might happen more and more frequently, with the little gray cells slipping away and making the wrong neural connections.

My tracking of my own personal deterioration, as I describe it, as it happens, may feel self-absorbed to you, even self-serving, but I am the only human being who really knows what's going on for me. Self-examination is often suspect, because we can't see ourselves with total objectivity—I know I cannot. But as I live and watch and write my record, I'm hoping for a kind of confessional honesty and transparency that will be essential if this document is to have value for me or anyone else. The transitions may be abrupt, unexpected, with surprising shifts and stops and starts, the way life is—every day different, like the weather in western Washington where I live.

I'm beginning to reflect on mortality, and the aging of mind and spirit that often precedes it—that universal end for which the scientists have, as yet, no answer, no solution. I will ask a succession of *whys* (why do we have to die? in fact, why were we born, why are we here at all?) and *whens* and *wheres* (both unanswerable) and *hows* (sudden death by accident or illness, or a slow kind of desiccation until all our vital juices are drained?). These are not new questions for the human race, but I'm asking them because they are *my* questions and I long for personal answers. Maybe you can profit from thinking about them as well.

# 2

# Looking Ahead

*No matter at what stage* of our journey, for each of us the inevitability of dying is always there, like the blank wall of an impenetrable fortress. Or an unexplored planet. Or a looming cliff face before us, with few visible toeholds.

The biblical prophets and teachers have claimed and proclaimed a certain knowledge of what lies beyond that impregnable barrier—a state of being either beatific or horrific. But where are the witnesses? A few have come back through some miraculous orifice in the rampart, but either we have no record of their comments (Lazarus) or they've been unable to describe in recognizable terms what they've seen and heard. Jesus was resurrected, having "harrowed hell," but what did that mean?

Many near-death experiences with visions of light or music or voices are documented. But since no one else can see or hear what's going on in that mysterious interim, we wonder—are these chemical or neurological reactions to the shutting down of our faculties? Is it a dreamlike state of wish fulfillment? Or is this a fore-view of heaven?

My guess is that what lies ahead is indescribable in human terms; that descriptions of heaven (or hell), as in Dante or Milton, are metaphorical attempts to translate a vision that came and went. Like the descriptions in the Revelation of a sea of glass and gates of pearl, and a river of life with leafy trees along its banks, and an open manuscript with lists of names of heavenly residents on it, and some sort of dwellings. (Will we need houses for privacy, or for shelter from celestial weather? I wonder if Jesus talked about the "many residences" being prepared for us to give us a sense of the reality and space of the heavenly community, along with some sort of continuity and familiarity that might be comforting.) But I wonder, will I like the decor, and will I get used to the other amenities? Is there a heavenly version of Scrabble with little ivory tiles and English letters? Myself, I'm hoping for an airy work space with lots of light and books and some flowering potted plants. And a PC that never gets obsolete.

Yet here's what Emily Dickinson, from her secluded nook in Amherst, suggested: "For Heaven is a different thing, / Conjectured, and waked sudden in— / And might extinguish me!"[1]

Andrew Hudgins surmises something far less overwhelming about those who look forward to living in heaven: "They'll talk of how they'll finally learn to play the flute / and speak good French. // Still others know they'll rot / and their flesh turn to earth, which will become / live oaks, spreading their leaves in August light."[2]

So for now we must do with hints and guesses—a collage of human hopes and dreams and uncertainties. We are left with a provisional present that is winding down like a loosened spring. That loosening is what I hope to describe, as long as I have any powers of description left.

# 3

# Feasting on Distances

*I'm writing about the process* of getting older, with the difficulties and deficits of age. I'm eighty-four, definitely on the uphill side, yet I'm so very glad I'm alive!

Reading Amy Frykholm's recent "contemplative biography" of Julian of Norwich, I came across this nugget from Julian's own writings: "God is being and wants us to sit, dwell and ground ourself [sic] in this knowledge while at the same time realizing that we are noble, excellent, assessed as precious and valuable and have been given creation for our enjoyment because we are loved."[1]

This is manifestly so for me, as on a clear day with the smell of frost in the air, when I feel exhilarated. The multiple tones of the color green do it for me. And all the other colors, and the textures and smells and sounds that bring my senses to full alert.

The arrival of a new idea or image for a poem propels me into such a fervor that my body tingles along with my mind. So much is wrong with the world, but so much of it is right, particularly the parts that seem to have spilled directly from the Creator's hand! What are the chances that when I was born I would turn out to be me, to have the astonishing chances and choices I've had? Beauty, in any form or color, makes me sing and have hope. Can I ever be thankful enough?

Though the struggles of living and survival have sometimes seemed unbearable, I've not been an unhappy woman. Growth and experience and the richness of creation have often brought me an intense joy in living. My five children and their own lively and intelligent offspring, and now my great-grandchildren, each such a distinct and gifted individual, have brought me all the joys and trials of parenting—a fullness of experience that I have never regretted. Matriarchy can be fun! Having had two faithful and supportive husbands in succession, men who put up with my ups and downs and always gave me the benefit of the doubt—how grateful I am for them! And my friends of the heart—my longtime camping/writing/knitting companion Karen, the prayer partners, Lydia, Marya, Claudia, Deb, Jennie, Bev, who meet in my study Monday mornings, all the fellow writers and artists whose helpful encouragement and critique have blessed me over the years—where would I have been without them?

*

What frees me most completely from the hindrances of physical disability is driving! My reflexes are still quick and reliable. My eyes are good enough. I hear well, except at a table with lots of other talkers all trying to make themselves heard. I'm a good and seasoned driver and I *love* cars. As the new models are introduced year by year, I learn to identify them and enjoy their sleek designs with excitement. I've had a love affair with automobiles, the movable domains for travel, ever since I bought my first Honda Accord after the death of Harold, my first husband and the father of my children. The car was a gently-used model, and my son Jeff helped me to find the auto dealership in downtown Chicago. The car had a stick shift, and I loved getting what was called "the feel of the road." Since then

I've had a string of Toyotas, Subarus, more Hondas and one small diesel-powered Nissan. I love the little pearly-green Prius I have now and feel noble and happy that its reduced emissions are not contributing too much to climate change.

Long distances are my joy—from Bellingham to California and back, camping along the way, relishing the sense that the hills and the green valleys and the lion-colored deserts of the continent are unrolling beneath my wheels hour after hour.

If I had the money, I'd get a canary-colored Ferrari with a gigantic spoiler. I'd own the road!

One of my fondest memories is driving cross-country from the West Coast to Chicago, and when near Sturgis, South Dakota, quite suddenly finding myself at the center of a fleet of motorcycles on their way to the annual Harley rally there. With their shiny black helmets and metal-studded leather jackets and gleaming, noir-ish hawgs, they looked like giant soldier ants. I was in the center of the pack, feeling as brave and proud as the four presidents carved there on the cliff face!

### Weight loss

*That bones will brittle*
*Is my truth,*
*And that all little*
*Cells, forsooth,*
*Will fail and fall,*
*And falling, leave*
*My brain's recall.*

*So I receive*
*Lightness of being,*
*And a beginning*
*Of agreeing*
*With this thinning.*

*So long, lucidity.*
*Welcome, life's*
*Gentle finality—*
*Its gradual knife.*

*Forgive the cells*
*That float and fly.*
*They've done quite well,*
*And so have I.*[2]

❧

We recently returned from a trip to the East Coast and a visit with Jeff and Donna and their blooming young family. We convoyed by car up from Connecticut to Rhode Island, where Jeff had rented a timeshare in Newport for a fortnight. The light feels different out there, particularly as we looked out on the Atlantic and basked in the heat of the midday sun. Jake and Ella had swimming lessons. I had a massage. We all went sailing on a sixty-foot yacht in the harbor, leased for a couple of hours, the children taking turns at the wheel and scampering along the deck to the bow. Excited. Unafraid. We walked along the seafront of the Breakers, famed for grand galas and the vacations of the wealthy in times past.

One memorable day John and I drove down to Ashaway to meet with some of my New England brothers- and sisters-in-law at a seafood restaurant. We all agreed, there's nothing quite like New England clam chowder made with butter and cream! We passed around family photos and reminisced about Cape Cod holidays back in the 1950s and 60s. These Shaws are all in their late eighties and nineties, ahead of me in years and faith, and they keep going with fortitude and good humor. The fact that we could all be together in one place before we die was singularly meaningful.

~~~~

In a poem in *Image*, Christian Wiman writes about "feasting on distances, gazing / dead into the sun." That sounds absolutely right—to look ahead to a far horizon with confidence, without flinching or fear; to let myself be gloriously blinded with possibility. I would like to infect my contemporaries, both young and old, with an openness that frees us to talk about unknowns, muscled by faith, with joy as fluid in me as the blood in my veins. Feasting on distances. Yes.

# 4

## Fit for the Climb?

*I'm developing a kind of* morbid fascination with my body. My hair is thinner. My stylist kindly rebukes me: "Not thinner, dear. Softer." It's a mix of gray and white, and my kids (four of whom are in their fifties) are adamant that I shouldn't color it. I like it that my eyebrows and eyelashes are still dark enough to give my face some character.

I've shrunk in height about an inch and a half from early adulthood, but my weight has stabilized to a comfortable 140 pounds. Yet when I look in the mirror my face looks leaner and bonier. Sagging is happening; unfortunately, it's not symmetrical. Sometimes when I see myself in the morning I think I look quite lovely; other times my mother's ancient face looks back at me. No matter how much moisturizing lotion (anti-aging, anti-wrinkle, collagen-supplying, sun-protecting, expensive) I apply each morning, as the skin shrinks over time it loses its lovely elasticity. The creases and furrows gather, gently pleated and folded and soft. In my left cheek there's a tiny bulge; when I finger it I can feel my pulse there. An artery under the skin? If I mention cosmetic surgery—just the idea; I doubt if I'd ever feel justified in spending money on something so artificial—my prayer friend Deb sounds horrified as she declares: "No! You've *earned* every one of those wrinkles."

Somehow the idea of being a landmark for a hard-working life should seem more appealing. The idea of "aging gracefully" sounds like a positive but feels like a capitulation. Dylan Thomas, raging against the dying of the light, certainly thought so. Yet somehow we can't stop fighting the deterioration, all the while knowing it's a losing battle. It's the push and pull of it that leaves us quivering in the interim.

But then I wonder, what gives me a right to feel cheated, defrauded of my capabilities as they drift away? Even though I didn't plan it or choose it, is being alive and human a right, or a privilege, or a life sentence? My knee joints are constructs of ceramic and titanium. They feel strong, and that gives me confidence when walking or standing, though hiking or climbing up- or downhill is wearisome. My left ankle has been surgically "replaced"—the whole joint taken apart and cleaned of bone chips and spurs from the strenuous efforts of my athletic youth— I was a high-jumper, a swimmer, a wilderness canoeist, a springboard diver and a basketball player—and has been strengthened and stabilized with six steel pins.

I consider this reconstruction a minor miracle. I can walk without a limp or a sharp pain in the joint. But my body is now artificial enough to invariably set off the alarms at airport security stations, which qualifies me for what I confess is a rather comforting dose of human touch. Being patted down in the discreet way the TSA people have been trained to feel bodies and detect certain foreign objects—I've decided to view the process, even the newly required "enhanced patdowns," as a series of gentle love pats. Even the machines that "enhance" the body image feel like an affirmation, as I am declared passable.

I'm beginning to see my body as landscape, full of contrast and light and shade. Why would I not want my physical self, even my facial muscles, to tell the truth about me? Why bother to pretty it up? Why color my hair or paint my nails? Why try to deceive or cover up my deficiencies with makeup?

I lift up my arm, alarmed at the slack flesh that hangs from it like a curtain, signifying that my canoeing muscles have atrophied. I look at my hands and feet, at the thin, age-mottled skin that is transparent enough to be a parchment map of veins and bony peaks and valleys among the metatarsals. In spite of its sheerness, the skin looks chalky. Even in bright light nothing reflects from it; there is no body oil to shine. Bruises appear out of nowhere, perhaps because I take a daily baby aspirin as a blood thinner.

The finger knuckles, arthritic, my mother's legacy that I'm already passing on to my daughters, are swollen so that I can't remove my gold wedding ring and the engagement ring with the sapphire we got in Israel. I've tried lubricating that fourth finger on the left hand with soap or oil or lotion. I've tried holding my hand high in the air to drain it of blood. All to no avail.

### Old hand

*The plum blue veins embroider their way*
*through a shrinkage of tissue, a lacing*
*of vines sucking at an unseen reservoir.*
*I touch my parchment skin, pushing it sideways*
*with the tentative forefinger of the other hand*
*and the pale tendons gleam like ivory*
*over the backdrop of murky muscle.*
*Across a keyboard the fingers flicker,*
*dedicated, busy with words that are concentrating*
*on imaginings larger than hinged metacarpals*
*or a minor mountain range of knuckles.*
*Made for work, curving to the keys, necessary adjuncts*
*to language, bridges from the brain.*[1]

I like my rings. I don't want to get rid of them. But they hug me too tenaciously. If I have to have more surgery, the techs will have to remove the rings by sawing them off. This is the physical evidence not of illness but of mortality. And there are other things that will have to go.

Freedom from pain and awkwardness is a wonderful thing, but it doesn't stand alone. It implies release *from* something or *toward* something. From pain to relief. From gravity to levity. From depression to exhilaration. From restriction to release.

Without restriction and struggle, freedom would have little meaning. If freedom were all we had, it would seem insignificant. Case in point: after six months of internal combustions, my gut spasming and liquefying most of what I eat, I am finally experiencing freedom from the symptoms. My gastroenterologist, Dr. Stiner, the one who administers those heavenly colonoscopies, after extensively testing me has decided, as he put it, to treat me "empirically rather than scientifically," using a pricey medication imported from Europe. (I always enjoy talking to Jane, the doctor's nurse, who greets me with "Well, if it isn't the lovely Luci!" Jane has an uncanny ability to relate to all the doctor's numerous patients like real people. Comforting.)

In the context of my internal upheavals, I love Julian of Norwich's observation so neatly and succinctly put: "A man walks upright, and the food in his body is shut in as if in a well-made purse. When the time of his necessity comes, the purse is opened and then shut again, in most seemly fashion. And it is God who does this, as it is shown when he says that he comes down to us in our humblest needs" (Long Text 6). This seems as if it should be in the GI textbook for student internists.

God's compassionate care even extends to the design and routine of our bodily functions. I feel so much perkier now that I can transpose my discomfort and dysfunction into the image of me as an ostrich-leather Gucci purse with a gold-plated snap that opens and shuts.

I'm thrilled at how one normal BM a day feels like liberation!

~~~

Forgetfulness is the throbbing fear of the elderly. We develop our little systems to deal with it. Always leave your car keys hanging on the hook beside the door into the garage. Always put your sunglasses in the same pocket in your purse. Always take your pills, all fifteen of them, first thing when you get up. And all the other meds when you go to bed. Remember to answer those emails, and pay the bills before the due date. Get your driver's license renewed (but study the new rules of the road first). Make that return phone call. Take your prayer book to church. Wash and dry those jeans that you plan to wear tomorrow on your trip. Put your boarding pass and passport where you can get at them easily at check-in.

Trust that your little brain cells keep up the good work, organizing the rest of your body for life and survival!

~~~

So much for the body, the temporary house in which we exist. But what about the thrust of spirit for survival and individuation that seems to dwell in all forms of life? In the human being it's honed to a fine point by consciousness and self-consciousness.

I'd have hoped that by now in my life some questions would have been resolved. I think with amazement of the distance I have traveled from my very conservative early indoctrination in Christian theology and practice. I still hold the name Christian, but what meaning does that designation carry anymore? It's a label that has become generic, too broad in its application to do much but distinguish its adherents from those with a Jewish or Islamic or other religious heritage. To say I'm a follower of Christ gets at the heart of it, but what a failing follower I am! It is pure grace that I feel assured and reassured of my place in Christ's body.

What is grace? What is inevitability? Where have all my searchings led me, even with the occasional epiphany (though I might have anticipated that epiphanies would be a thing of the past)? George MacDonald, in *The Wise Woman*, suggested that with age the evidences and illuminations from beyond us will become less frequent, less clear. That the unknowns would gather like rain clouds.

I'm pondering the ultimate despair of mortality. (And the word *pondering* implies weight; this is a heavy theme.) If one is being, like me, carried on a slow train toward death, a nonbeing of bodily life and perhaps of the essential soul—what is the point of all the accumulation of human existence? All the achievement of ecstatic moments, the repeated fulfillment of desires and needs? The occasional relief of release after tension and anxiety? Of satisfaction after hunger? Of pleasure? Of all the beauty and creative work of artists of all time? Of the skills developed— writing, gardening, knitting, typing, photography?

Of what value is the growth of a body of wisdom that life and learning have achieved in us? All the fertile pockets of experience translated into words and images and letters and messages, each longing for some kind of permanence—the preservation of emotion and illumination in a discrete expression that holds it up to view in its own clear cell of a written form?

I keep a reflective journal. I write poems and essays that attempt to capture and hold on to insight and experience. I take photographs to keep memories alive and to refine and express my sense of beauty and design. Everyone now has a point-and-shoot camera or a smartphone that can snap and save an image. Now there are so many trillions of such images that when we're gone, who'll care?

I'll be beyond caring! In my attic hundreds of carousels of slides have lain waiting to be viewed, images of our entire family growth over sixty years. My family says they'd love to see them on the screen, but who has a projector anymore? My brother is endeavoring to transfer them all onto CDs for us. But is anyone really interested in looking at them? It will be ancient history and obsolete technology, likely to be relegated to the trash heap, the burn pile of trivialities.

What about all the challenges I've taken up and succeeded at? The risks I've taken? The failures I've learned from? Is that set down in that record book in heaven for safekeeping? Have I accomplished anything of lasting worth? Even more intimately delicate is the question, does it really matter what anybody thinks about me or my work?

What is the meaning and value of an insight gained, of a perception captured, along with perhaps some grains of wisdom? Even if it has been shared with kindred spirits, might it not evaporate in a swirl of someone else's forgetfulness and the swift passage of time?

What lasts, even for a lifetime? Is anything permanent? Books and magazines are being digitized, but with the rapid progress of technology much will become obsolete with time. Memory can become a prism through which to view the colorful events and accumulations of a long life. But what if the prism is shattered? What if the light is snuffed out like a candle flame? Is anything left but a dead wick?

~

My struggle with the large questions of the universe and my own wavering small life of faith has been brewing on and off all my life. The incarnation (such a fruitful source of poetry for me),

the miracles of Jesus, the mystery of the Trinity, the whole
concept of the transcendent as proclaimed by the church sometimes seem so arbitrary, so improbable in the light of contemporary scientific knowledge. Add to that the flaws and failings
of Christian believers, all of us tainted to some degree. Is this
what the body of Christ is supposed to look like?

I sometimes try to step back out of my own training and the
tight Christian system of belief. Even if we all search, how do we
*know*? I cannot know for sure, cannot assemble anything coherent and consistent in my mind except my longing for reality.
My lifelong commitment, reached again and again in this repeated quandary, is to *not give up on believing*.

One Sunday I felt a change coming. During the Scripture
readings and Fr. Jonathan's sermon I began to feel my spirit lift
in response. Perhaps part of this was my return to better health
after the miserable bout with diverticulitis during which I'd felt
bad enough to not care a heck of a lot whether I lived or died!

Then, this morning, a blue, sunny day, a surge of vigor and re-
solve and the sight through our bedroom window of vivid greens
and a purple finch in the cedars made me realize how utterly improbable is our entire planet, its richness and complexity, the marvel
of human intelligence and ingenuity, with its growing sophistication
and problem-solving ability. Its systems of reproduction and growth.
And if that seems unique and improbable in the known universe,
why should God's putting on skin and bone and talking our language and making friends and disturbing the status quo so that
miracles can become the order of the day be so hard to believe?

～

"The deeper it gets, the darker it gets." I quote from Fr. Dave
Denny, the worship leader at the Glen Workshop in Santa Fe.

Dave is a good friend, a hermit who lives in the Colorado desert. A scholar, poet and old soul with whom I've partnered from time to time leading worship with MFA classes on Whidbey Island. His own story is shadowed by past conflicts and searchings. He admits to a lack of certainty that translates into an openness to further revelation, and because of that I find it easy to make personal admissions to him about faith and my lack.

We were talking about spiritual direction, which he is offering to anyone so inclined at St. John's College in Santa Fe, the site of annual workshops for artists and writers. He prefers the term "soul friendship," which implies a relationship of mutuality, a giving and taking, rather than a one-way street of counseling. I seem to be approaching this mutuality in my own relationship with my soul friend Barb Pal, who has frequently saved me from my despair with myself and God over the last twelve years.

In the past I've disclosed to Dave some of the uncertainties I've been plowing through—the existential questions that seem to cling to my mind like dark tar. These queries of the universe have plagued me, pestered me for so many years, and I doubt that they will ever truly leave me alone. Skepticism about God—is he good? loving? personal?—haunts me like a shadow over my face. Is this the result of wondering too often and knowing too much? I think of Isaiah, a prophet whose visions and predictions alternated between catastrophe and glory. Even he could say, perplexed, "Truly, you are a God who hides himself" (Isaiah 45:15).

Some of my bewilderments and doubts may have come from my weekly times with my prayer group at home, along with searching souls like Bev and Lydia who have left fundamentalist Christianity behind and sense God, in a mystical way, in and beyond and through creation. They seem to have found some tranquillity as they believe in a universe larger and more harmonious than that of common Christian faith. There are times when this seems appealing, until I remember the ongoing crises of humanity, and then the tenets of my own shreds of belief cling to me, and I to them.

Dealing with doubt. In spite of a sense of spiritual renewal, the scars of this old wound of spirit keep breaking open to reveal raw pain. Or sometimes its opposite—the numbness to sensation after a cut has severed the nerves.

Often I think of myself as weak or lazy in relying on the assurance of others about the reality of God to bolster my own wavering convictions.

Nevertheless, I find myself returning again and again to a center sought in God, making a decision of will: to seek to renew my faith and put doubts aside. To allow some of my existential questions to remain unanswered.

*I will believe*
*until my will to believe*
*takes hold, unmakes me,*
*my unbelief swallowing itself*
*the way a dimming sun*
*swallows a shadow.*

I determine to propel myself into the mysteries of faith by going through the motions and words of the liturgy.

It seems fruitless to keep dithering, switching back and forth between faith and unfaith like a pair of abandoned tennis shoes swaying in the wind, strung by their shoelaces from a telephone wire.

Evelyn Underhill, in *The Mystery of Sacrifice*, lent to me by my church friend Stacy, says this: "[The Eucharist's] ritual actions provide . . . an impersonal frame in which the most secret responses of the spirit to God can find shelter and support."

So the physical "accidents" of place, time, location, relationship give me reason to return. Even bodily actions like kneeling or crossing oneself, or cradling two hands together to receive the body of Christ, or lifting one's lips to the edge of the chalice and taking a sip of that wine, dark and bitter as blood, can become substrates, springboards that lift bread and wine into an arena where eventually we find ourselves in God's presence, partaking of his love in an almost tangible way. In that place perhaps all questions become irrelevant. Perhaps we will know as we are known—utterly, cleanly, clearly.

I've determined to mobilize expectant trust.

～

Jennie, a dear friend, after receiving disappointing news in a job search during a time of financial stress, told me that as she was walking in the woods yesterday, half-praying, half-wondering and questioning God, she noticed on the forest track a smooth, round pebble. It wasn't on a beach or by a river, but unaccountably nestled all by itself in the center of a hiking trail. Like me, she notices things, picks up stones. This one had quartz inclusions striping horizontally and vertically across the gray stone, forming a perfect cross. "It was like an immediate answer from God. A gift." She knew that God was with her, even on this muddy track of her life.

Then today, a gift for me. After Chinese takeout, the fortune cookie disclosed the usual slip of paper, but with these words: "Do you believe? Your endurance and persistence will be rewarded." I know how bland and obvious these little axioms usually are. But in this day in my life it was meaningful. I'm even applying it to the writing of this chronicle of my later life. (My friend Madeleine L'Engle, on being presented with a fortune-cookie truism, would always add, "in bed," to the accompaniment of hysterical laughter.)

These small instances, these incidents of the felt presence of God made known to us in mysterious ways, tell me I am not alone.

In church yesterday, letting my questions fall away, I felt a strong urging to enter the worship liturgy without reservation. To let the words and music resonate with meaning—the result, I think, of my renewed decision to leave unanswerable questions unanswered, to feel the barriers to belief being gently dismantled. To discern in the Scripture lessons messages to take to heart. To sing the hymns burnished into familiarity and reflect on the remarkable insights of their writers and composers and allow praise to take root in me.

And then I yearned to take the wafer and wine with an open heart. I was eager to go, thankful and fulfilled, to the side altar and there to lay hands on and pray with those who came for healing. I could deeply believe that God was joining me and my healing partner in prayer to respond to heartfelt needs. I could hear words I hadn't planned pouring from my own lips, and felt myself to be a link between love and need. The Spirit at work.

❧

*The wind blows wherever it pleases*
*How secretly the bones move*
*    under the skin*
*and the veins thread their way*
*    through their forests, the trees*
*of bones, the mosses of cells,*
*    the muscle vines.*
*How privately the ears*
*    tune themselves to music heard*
*only in the echoing cave of the head.*
*    And the tongue in its grotto tests*
*the bitterness of unripe fruit, and wine,*
*    the mouth feel of honey*

*in the comb. How cunningly our shadows*
  *follow us as we walk.*
*And our breath, how it moves in*
  *and out without great thought.*
*Even rain, which needs no summons from us*
  *but flows, a gift from heaven,*
*as the grasses rise greenly, shivering.*
  *Just so, beauty besieges us*
*unannounced, invading us, saving our souls.*
  *So it is with the Spirit.*[2]

⁓

I'm feeling some release from my unrealistic expectations of myself. The crowd of unanswerable questions that has plagued me for so long felt like a cage, imprisoning me from the freedom of full faith. I am realizing now that no matter how intelligent and persistent I may be, I'm unlikely to find all the ultimate answers in this life.

This allows me a new freedom in worship. I hope to perceive my life as increasing in health and well-being in spite of the depredations of age.

William Sloan Coffin once said, "I love the recklessness of faith. First you leap, and then you grow wings." I long to leap. I want to feel the stirrings of wing feathers from my shoulder blades.

⁓

Like Jesus, the Word embodied in real flesh, his word to us is embodied in symbols. I look to crosses, to candles, to stained-glass windows, to incense, to icons, to poems, even to fiction and stories in news magazines, to remind me of unseen realities.

Words call out to me from a page, provoking new thinking. I
need reminders, and may need them more and more with aging.

～

The chameleon effect again. I still feel split sometimes, having all
the right Christian responses, behaviors and language, then stepping
back out of myself to ask: *Do I really, wholeheartedly believe this?*

It's too late in my life to change in any radical way. My knee-
jerk theology, pretty orthodox and complete, is in the forefront
of my life. It has firm hold of me.

Yet how fond I am of the word *liberal* and its cognate cousins
*liberty* and *liberation*, all detached from their religious and political
connotations and enlarging on the idea of freedom. In the quiet of
some early morning's light, seen through my bedroom window, the
diminutive bodies of chickadees often whip from tree to tree so
fluidly and with such ease, liberated. Geese, advertising their
presence with the familiar honks, form a V over the lake and are
gone in a moment, free to fly north or south as the seasons dictate.

Often, in my morning pondering, while I'm still in bed and de-
bating whether to get up or lie there just a few more minutes, ideas
fly through my mind like a moving cloud of winged creatures.

～

One year I was asked to introduce Eugene Peterson as he received the Denise Levertov Award in Seattle. In preparation I
reread much of his writing and felt the central strength of his
conviction, expressed so freshly and vividly, and could align
myself with it at the time. On my own, the spiritual foundation
sometimes wobbles and gives way. I'm guilty of flip-floppery and
hobby-horsery. I'd like to clone myself and start over, 100 percent

fresh and willing, a blank slate for God to write on. But he seems to have had other plans! He knows my heart, my longing for truth. I trust that and manage to work up some gratitude.

～

W. H. Auden, in his poem "Archeology," reflects on what the archaeologist may find, and concludes:

*Knowledge may have its purposes,*
*but guessing is always more fun*
*than knowing.*

In the context of this poem, writer Scott Cairns reflects that "perplexity is, at the very least, preferable to an array of clear, comprehensible, and *mistaken* certainties."[3] Which makes a strong case for the merits of ambiguity and paradox. Speaking of comfort, I find this comforting (strengthening), realizing, as I do every day, that in this life any certainty is a myth, and that those who erect the houses of their lives on certain "certainties" may very well be in for the catastrophe of a landslide down a very steep hill. I recall Jesus saying something very similar about buildings and foundations.

So how do I know what I know? And how sure can I be of what I think I know? Once again I am thrust into mystery. Poet Anne Sexton pictured her faith as hanging from a very thin thread. My life is too short and my connections too limited for profound knowledge, let alone wisdom.

The presence of paradox deepens the mystery. In Scripture the Lamb and the Lion represent one and the same person. We live by faith but must not neglect works—Paul and James have always seemed a bit at odds to me. We believe in the super-natural but have to make the decisions and choices dictated by our very natural lives; we hover between heaven and earth.

I once wrote a poem, "Amphibian," about the life of a frog. Caught between water and air, he needs oxygen to breathe, but diving down, being immersed in pond water, keeps his skin from drying out and cracking. At the time it was my metaphor for the life of the Christian—drawn toward the air and freedom of heaven, yet with earthy mortal bodies to harbor our souls and keep us earthbound.

✎

I'm convinced of the inevitability of my own aging, the ongoing diminishment of my responses to the world, my becoming as limited as a child again but without a child's wide horizon of life ahead of me. Yet when I think of my children, and the children of my friends, all of them in vibrant midlife, midflight, their own inevitable aging and death feel incomprehensible. They are all so creative, vital, contributors to life rather than consumers. I can't imagine them with wrinkles, unlucky bones, sluggish paces—though on a couple of heads a few gray hairs are sprouting like unwelcome weeds in a field! And a head of hair or two are getting thin!

✎

On a TV news channel I listened to an interview with an inventor, a man whose own legs had been amputated, and who with many false starts has finally designed for himself prosthetic legs of metal and plastic with intricate connections to the nerves in his torso and upper body. He says with a grin, "Though the rest of me is getting older, my artificial legs are upgradable, and they're getting better and better!"

# 5

# Dangers Ahead?

*If I sometimes sound cynical,* bear with me. I'm fighting an existential battle against annihilation.

It's a summer evening, and a blue bottle fly is frantically orbiting the room, noisily bumping into the window glass and glancing off the light shade in unwieldy circuits. What is his point? Is he looking for a place to land? Please, not on me. But his flight is ceaseless. Is his reason for being any more significant than mine—both of us creatures with sparks of life?

When I opened the screen door and moved out onto the deck one recent morning, I was immediately ambushed by spider silk; I couldn't tell where it had come from, and it felt sticky, creepy, lacing my face and in my hair. While I admire spiders for the way they spin their fiercely strong filaments from their own bodies, I realize I'm fairly arachnophobic.

In my early childhood in the south of England, in Surrey, I remember walking into an outsized web suspended on a shrub in our back garden, and feeling horrified and weirdly panicked that something I could barely see was enveloping me. I would have hoped to have outgrown such feelings. What other vulnerabilities from my early childhood persist to haunt me? I was held to a very high standard of behavior and performance, and sometimes fear of criticism or rebuff still feels like a clinging web across my plans.

⁂

Anxiety. Sometimes it rises in my throat with a sour taste. The problem is, none of us knows how long we have left. Or what physical problems will afflict us. Will our money last? That's one question, but not the most important. There is so much I hope yet to do, to learn, to experience (though once again, why is that important to anyone but me?). Can I trust that God will allow me enough energy and length of days to realize and carry out my calling and complete the climb?

⁂

I was raised in the constant dread about the second coming of Christ to "catch away" God's redeemed people. In that setting one had to be sure one had sincerely, and from the bottom of one's heart, accepted Jesus as Lord and Savior. As a five-year-old and on into preadolescence, I did this again and again, hoping I'd perfected the formula, with the right sequence of words and depth of feeling, to make very sure. I was scared to death of the consequences of failure.

I had a terrible fear of abandonment, that Mum and Dad would be raptured and I'd be left, and then what would I do, dreadfully young, unprepared, all alone in an alien world? For years I'd creep into their room at night to hear their breathing, almost giddy with relief at my dad's resonant snores and my mother's steady breath sounds or slight movements. My Christianity was born out of fear of abandonment rather than a feeling that God loved me and longed for me to love him. I don't think that was the legacy my devout parents hoped for. But that's what it felt like, a dread that visits me still in dreams.

So. Multiple questionings and a few answers—some that begin to satisfy, others that remain open ended.

≈

Information overload. We seem to be spending more and more time in social networking, hooked to our machines. I'd feel lost without email. I got snared into Facebook a few months ago and am amazed at what personal trivia people think it worthwhile to post. *Headache tonight. Maybe some milk and a cookie before bed. Hung out with my sister. Etc., etc.* But then some thoughtful, truly informative comment or posting sends my own thinking in a fruitful direction, and I'm grateful.

≈

A recent *Time* magazine article reported on a new device under development, a sort of digital super-guide in the form of a tiny corneal lens that informs you where the nearest post office or pizza joint is, who that man is just ahead of you on the sidewalk, how far it is to the bus stop. Technically this is to be known as an "Internet-enabled contact lens to allow simultaneous engagement in real and virtual worlds." The maps can fall from your hands. You can know, instantly, where you are wherever you are.

Soon none of us will need cameras or global positioning devices—our brains will receive the information we need simply by following the thread of a mental whim or question. Meaningful conversations will likely lag. We'll know instantly what our friends are thinking or plotting. Words will fall out of fashion. Information will fill us with instant trivia. I hope I die first.

While I sometimes lament the artificiality that seems to creep in with technological innovation, I am grateful for the attention that is being paid today to the possibilities of digitizing our reading materials, of increasing the speed of our interhuman communication. We can hear words through the empty air; we can almost see ideas as they are translated into images on the screen. But I'm especially captured by what Tina Brown, in *Newsweek*,[1] calls "the interpretive pleasure of the printed page."

Again and again I'm flabbergasted by the power of language, of words—those little dark scribbles on a paper page, or hieroglyphics on a clay tablet or on parchment, or the tanned skin of an animal, and now on tablets that miraculously download stored writings—their power to carry a thought through thousands of years and into our minds in the present, presenting a contemporary correlative to an ancient question or complexity or issue in human life.

It's as if the ancient bardic oracles and songs and oral histories and warrior shouts needed more than the air to carry the messages. The thoughts held enough power to need some permanence, some transmitting wire, some way of getting through to other human beings no matter how far into the future, some way of informing us, "This idea is burning in my own mind. Here, let me light a wick in you."

Because of this the words of God didn't get lost. Like stones thrown into a pond, their ripples keep washing our shores today.

I read and read and read, and my mind is full of the old and repeated cries of the ancients, which haven't changed that much, except for the speed at which they can be conveyed. Did Dante, Shakespeare or Milton suspect this? Did Socrates, Plato, Euripides and other ancient philosophers have a clue that their ideas would still live, and be read and learned from and endlessly discussed in our century? Did Aquinas and Origen and Polycarp and Irenaeus have any idea how powerfully they would influence theology centuries later?

⁂

The clouds and chill are back after a week-long heat wave. It's as if heaven has been cut off and obscured. I'm feeling depressed and finding it hard to sleep, even though I'm tired. My mind keeps grinding out words and ideas. Sometimes these seem meaningful, but often they feel disconnected and fruitless.

Dreams seem to be vividly colorful and more absurd than usual, involving frustrations, often about cars that break down and searches for something elusive. Often it's feeling unprepared for an upcoming exam, or being unable to find my college dorm room in an enormously complicated multistoried brick building, or failing to find my car in a parking lot at the airport. Generally I wake from such a dream with a sense of intense anxiety and inadequacy. I dream intensely nearly every night.

I know how impossible it is in the cold reality of morning to describe one's own improbable dream to someone else. The images and events morph so oddly into each other. I see colors I've never seen when I'm awake, seemingly part of a different spectrum. People from my earlier life reappear. Some of them seem to betray me, others to protect and accompany me on wild forays into a dream world that is, quite literally, fantastic. I'm often naked below (or above) the waist, and fleeing from danger. Sometimes there are good dreams in which my husbands are present together—relating quite amicably, as befits the behavior of faithful Christian men.

Strangely enough, the dreams return again and again to certain "pseudogeographical" locations that fray at the edges and seem to bleed into each other. For example, an enormous and complex high school with multiple entrances outside one of which I've parked my car. Not only can I hardly ever remember which floor my classroom is in, or which stairs to take, or which flight of back stairs to avoid, but when I do find the room my classmates are already halfway through a test for which I haven't studied. Utter panic results.

Another setting is in West Chicago, where we built a home on the prairie back in the 1950s. I can see the green swell of the grass and driveway leading from it, opening down into a long steep hill with street car tracks that end up being in Toronto. I have a vehicle of some sort—not a car, a species of motorcycle that looks like a large mosquito that needs gas and constantly veers into the wrong lane against my will. And invariably I've lost the ignition key.

At one end of that Midwestern dream house there's a suite of lavish rooms accessed through winding corridors that in my dreams I rarely visit. It is decorated in a rich, ornate style quite foreign to me, and seems to be being saved for some future festive event or distinguished guest. Is this a premonition of heaven? Or of entry into richer life in God? Fertile fields and forests surround the house, and an unpaved track through a meadow that leads to a view of a mountain range in Australia. You have to enter a circuitous tunnel to get to the highest peak, where an elegant lunch will be served, and photo ops of vast distances abound. After that you can hike along a river, and you end up floating down it pleasurably to where it ends in a roaring semicircular waterfall. There are no warning signs, but you know you need to scramble out of the river before it breaks into this cataract.

How does real life influence dream life? Is it all just a series of chemical and neurological reactions? What fears are translated by the dreaming imagination into pictures of dread or pleasure, or escape or adventure? I know there are principles to the interpretation of dreams, and I wish I had a handle on them. But in this arena of my mind, mystery still reigns. What is my brain saying that my conscious mind can't pin down? Or is there a connection? Sometimes dreaming seems to clarify, but so often my dreams leave me baffled.

⁂

Today at our church Alms Ministry, we saw nineteen people. They come to St. Paul's for any kind of help we can offer— information about where to get a free shower, a meal, a place for the night, a bus ticket to Seattle, a recommendation for a clean and sober house. Often they are out of work and their power has been cut off; can we give them enough money for another month's warmth and light? Our resources are limited in a time of economic recession, but we hear stories that imprint us deeply and stay with us all week, until the next group shows up.

One week two brothers come together. We ask them to sit down with us so we can hear their story. One, the deaf one, can drive. The other, too weak to speak for himself, is scheduled for a heart operation in Seattle later in the week. They have an ancient Chevy but no money for gas. We give them a voucher for thirty dollars made out to a local gas station.

The relief on their faces, even tears! The driver sobs, looking at us and hugging his brother, "Thank you. He's all I've got." Fuel for a car, even an old, beat-up vehicle, is like the living soul in an aged body. It speaks of freedom, of forward momentum, of release, of hope, of possibility.

⁂

Walking from kitchen to office one morning, I felt my left knee suddenly buckle, as if it were going to bend backward instead of forward. It was painful, an odd, disturbing feeling. I worked away in my study on emails for a while, and when I got up again the knee was fine.

It was as if it had just sent me a sly reminder—a hint that I must treat it with respect because it threatens to get creakier with time. The way all of me will, all over. But oh, Lord, preserve my mind from creakiness for now!

꩜

Bev was here this morning, as usual for our prayer time on Mondays. She is one of my few remaining friends of the same generation, so we were opining and guessing together about the meaning of our existence. She noted that in both men and women the charts all show the sharp physical decline that begins with menopause and middle age, and the resulting retreat downhill. The downward curve is sharp, almost elbow-shaped. Bev contests this vigorously, convinced that from now on it is all *uphill,* never a tumble "over the hill." With ongoing life we should expect expansion, not diminution. So it's a steep slope all right, but it curves up, not down. Like an upended hockey stick.

This is encouraging!

# 6

## Finding Sure Footing

*Often I think of myself* as weak or lazy in relying on the conviction of others about the reality of God to bolster my own wavering convictions. In my faith, am I building on a rock or on a slippery beach that reconfigures itself every time the tide changes? Maybe something in between—sandstone, friable and artfully inscribed by water and weather, yet ground away under my restless feet and the sculpting of centuries, eons.

I find I vacillate between two extremes. One is a sense of personal inadequacy, the conviction that any success I've had in public life is an accident; that I am utterly undeserving. That all my efforts amount to wood, straw, hay, stubble, and what a blazing bonfire that will make when it is consumed! I expect very little gold or silver to be refined out from that purifying flame. My other recognition is that I have gifts given me without my asking that have brought me and others a modicum of satisfaction as I employ them.

I struggle with ambition, the hope that something I've contributed to the world has lasting value, and might even be unique, what no one else has done or could have done.

I know I need to love and value myself as God loves and values me. But I'm becoming increasingly wary of narcissism and self-absorption.

Evelyn Underhill, in *The Mystery of Sacrifice,* about the sacrament of the Eucharist, talks about "learning to break the barriers
of self-love." Miroslav Volf voices a similar principle, that of self-
donation, in his astonishing book *Exclusion and Embrace.* Though
this abolishment of narcissism may seem to be a fruitful process
for the good of the soul, it seems endlessly elusive, almost unachievable. Self-love and confidence are so central to human survival, and without a measure of self-love, a sense that our lives have
meaning and purpose and that we've been created for a reason, we
might be forgiven for asking the question "What's the point?"

*≈*

Stephen Hawking, in his recent book *The Grand Design,*
claims that a Creator wasn't necessary for the development of a
universe and solar system. I don't pretend to understand the
physics by which he reached this conclusion (years ago I read *A
Brief History of Time* and thought, after I'd read a couple of
chapters, *Well, I think I grasped his line of thought,* though like
most everybody else I can't recall his reasoning after the fact). It
seems ironic that this brilliant geophysicist, helplessly slumped
in his wheelchair, his body crippled by ALS, unable to speak
without an artificial voice-production device, utterly dependent
on others for daily existence, is in essence dismissing an all-
powerful force and source of life.

"Nothing comes from nothing, nothing ever could . . ." from
*The Sound of Music* keeps throbbing in my inner ears.

*≈*

Sundays, I'm often joined at the Mary Altar (at one side of the
church nave—known as the "healing rail" in our church) by

seekers and others needing God's help for their spirits and bodies, and to intercede for others. We have wonderful traditional prayer-book prayers for such occasions, but I and whoever is my partner in this healing prayer ministry first ask God to be our hands and our hearts as we join in seeking divine help for those who kneel before us.

And in these moments the words of prayer come, arriving from beyond me and pouring out through my mouth and my hands, laid on the head or shoulders of someone with a deep need. I have a feeling that I am an aqueduct for healing in a way hard to describe. There is such freedom in being a link between human need and divine provision and promise, and those moments are when I am most aware of the presence of the Spirit in my life. I love to remember what Paul said about comfort and consolation: "All praise to . . . the God of all healing counsel! He comes alongside us when we go through hard times, and before you know it, he brings us alongside someone else who is going through hard times so that we can be there for that person just as God was there for us" (2 Corinthians 1:3-4 *The Message*).

This mystery of words is also present when I write poetry. The phrases and images come from God knows where, quite literally. I have learned to trust that process, which is part of the art of writing—the listening, the catching a word or phrase midflight, of recording it right away so that it doesn't vanish. Of seeing an image for the words to clothe. Of attaching it to other words to paint a picture for others to see and use their own creative imaginations to bring into reality. For me this is an affirmation that the Spirit is at work in our own human spirits to verify the truth of our experience and share it beyond ourselves.

On NPR today I heard some music by an Italian composer, written to express his longing to enter a realm of spiritual truth and mystery that seemed to elude him. The piece was titled *Come In,* a kind of invitation that I took to be personal for me. These clues come when I need them most yet least expect them.

It was as if God was saying to me, "You've tried so hard to feel my presence and invite me into your life, but all you have to do is 'come in' to my love." Like entering my warm home after a walk in the windy, penetrating cold. This felt immensely comforting and right. I am repeating it to myself like a mantra whenever I feel lonely or depressed. "Come in." Yes.

I need this kind of reminder again and again. Looking back to old encouragements and insights isn't enough; it must be present, ongoing.

# 7

# Bivouacking

*Camping with Karen at Baker Lake.* Karen and I have tent-camped every summer for the last sixteen years. It is a treat we give ourselves, homebodies, responsible wives and parents. We value both being together and celebrating our ability to exist in the wilderness. And we both like this kind of solitude and time for thinking and questioning.

One year we discovered a beautiful campground with no other humans visible (it was just after Labor Day, and the kids in camping families were all back in school). Through the fir trees there was a view of a pristine lake and the possibility of sighting the snowy mountains that we knew from previous experience were just north of us in the Cascade Range.

Just as we arrived at the tent site, rain started to fall. We hurriedly got the tent up, and then mounted Karen's vast blue tarpaulin over the camp table with tall steel stakes and tarp lines. (This is a task that takes superhuman intelligence, coordination and patience to accomplish.)

Johnny and Christa, my son and daughter-in-law, are willing to "camp rough" with only sleeping bags and tarp, and I have been accused of being a "geriatric camper" because I like a bit of fabric over my head when I sleep, and I prefer striking a match to light our Coleman lamp rather than rubbing two sticks together. But I do love the heavenly sound of rain falling on the tent at night, like small wet bullets, while inside we are snug and warm and dry in our sleeping bags.

Call Karen and me either idiots or intrepid wilderness women, but we've sometimes stayed out there in nonstop rain *for four or five days* before packing it in and giving up.

Actually we always have a lovely time. We read novels, knit, take naps in our reclining chairs, build campfires and light citronella candles to keep away the mosquitoes, grill steaks, drink red wine, write our journals and take photographs of moss and spider webs and the rain-patterned lake to our hearts' content. We engage in long discussions, philosophical, theological or practical, as we open up our lives to each other. I can tell Karen things I cannot disclose to anyone else. And vice versa. This is what I call heart friendship.

In spite of my arachnophobia, we find spiders to be a fruitful source of speculation on these camping excursions—the shape and skill of their webs, and the magical way a spider can spin a thread *horizontally* between trees fifteen or twenty feet apart. We wonder, what does that arachnid think of humans? Of us, and our odd activities?

### Novel

*I'm utterly engrossed in the turn of*
*plot when a young visitor shows up, strolling*
*down the page, halting briefly at an*
*interesting word ("limbo"). She is, quite literally,*
*small as a pinhead with eight tiny feathery*
*legs like bits of dust. And dust is her color;*

*I'm guessing that she's too babyish for flashy.*
*When she clambers behind the page edge*
*I turn the book over and there she is, outlined*
*against a patch of red on the cover. Evidently*

*finding celebrity endorsements uninspiring,*
*she rejoins me on the printed page, smaller*
*than the letter "o" in "on," on which she sits and*
*considers the impregnability of a preposition.*

*We read together for a while, stunned*
*by the power of fiction. I need to turn*
*the page, but I can't. She's still barricaded*
*in her "o," and it's against my principles*
*to squash a friend. I lay the book down, open.*
*Hours later I check back but she's gone, off*
*to think up her own plot, or plan her first web.*[1]

Together Karen and I once watched a yellow jacket expertly catch a moth, clip her wings and carry off her inert body, food storage for the wasp nest. In every arena of the natural world, destruction and reconstruction happen. As a part of the creation, I realize my body may become food for worms. And this actually feels hopeful rather than creepy.

Lots of knitting gets done on these retreats from city life. Last summer I mounted a full frontal attack on my then current knitting project—a brown wool sweater jacket that I hoped to wear when John and I were to fly to Europe. The photo of the finished garment that came with the instructions is attractive and doesn't look too complicated. But the directions are badly written and confusing, including a term that I was unfamiliar with—*wrap.* I'd googled it. No luck. Karen, my longtime co-knitter, couldn't enlighten me.

Earlier I'd searched old knitting books. Finally I gave in and went to the knit shop where I'd bought the yarn, and the knitter-in-residence explained to me what I needed to do. In essence, *wrap* means simply "make a new stitch." I've always known how to do that! Why didn't the knitting book just say that? Now

I've only got a sleeve to finish and buttons to sew on.

*Later at Baker Lake.* Finished sewing the seams on the brown cardigan last night, attaching the six wooden buttons down the front. It fits perfectly. I am so pleased. Something like this gives me immense satisfaction. It's so tangible, a palpable token of the weeks it took to knit it, of the puzzling out of the abstract instructions into a new reality, of every inch of yarn that passed through my fingers onto the needles, along with the emotions and events along the way, all knitted into it, gathering it into itself to make a complete garment the way each of us has gathered our lives into ourselves, stitch by stitch, row by row until we are whole and may somehow bring comfort to this cold world.

&#x2615;

John and have just made our lunch sandwiches. He makes the most obnoxious combinations! Today he had whole-wheat bread with peanut butter, turkey leftovers and English marmalade, the bitter kind made with Seville oranges.

We both love butter, lots of it. And cream, so guilt-making, so delicious. It was those sorts of enjoyments that brought John and me together—those and Marmite—but I'm not into combining savory and sweet the way he does. It's one of those little differences that go into making a marriage interesting.

These days John cooks dinner a couple of times a week, which is a delightful reprieve that leaves me an afternoon free, but sometimes it ends up being quite the all-day production for him. I tell my husband that, being an engineer, he should have no trouble following the instructions in a recipe. (Did I mention the time when the idea of "folding" beaten egg whites into a soufflé baffled him? The creation ended up about a half-inch thick, but still tasted yummy.) But he hasn't yet learned the peace of mind that comes with putting things away after using them, to keep the field of battle clear.

I usually start thinking about dinner around 4:30 p.m., and the ideas for a meal float together in my mind much in the same way that prayers and poems gather themselves, without a lot of anguish.

# 8

# Above the Tree Line

*Fall, and the vine maples* along the streets and walking trails are leaking away their green so that their genuine nature— the reds and oranges and pinks and even subtle lavenders—are showing up for what they were all along, thanks to photosynthesis. The special authenticity of foliage in its passage to capitulation. A parable of aging?

I think I'm learning to *inhabit* my mortality, feeling out its coastlines and islands and sounding its depth every day, in much the same way as John and I do when sailing our Catalina around Puget Sound and the San Juan Islands. The weather conditions change as well as the topography. Tides sweep in and out at different levels. What I'm accustomed to today may have shifted tomorrow.

Or the "angle of repose," to use Wallace Stegner's term, may have been upended as internal eruptions take place in our emotional, spiritual or physical life.

Sometimes these changes feel volcanic and worrisome, as when my bladder doesn't heed my command to hang tight and I'm caught, embarrassingly, rushing for the nearest public bathroom in town and leaking along the way. Is this to be expected, and what am I to do about it?

Oh, I know. Talk to my doctor about this or that prescription for "overactive bladder," a euphemism suggested to help one feel less mortified about bodily urgings: it's my bladder, not me, that needs help.

Atul Gawande's articles in *The New Yorker* are always thought-provoking. Recently this physician-journalist wrote the essay "Letting Go," about how doctors can help their patients in the process of dying. A reader responded, quoting the final words of Stonewall Jackson as an example of "a good death." On the Lord's Day, the day of Jackson's dying, he said: "Let us cross over the river and rest under the trees."[1]

There's much about that kind of vision that appeals to me. It sounds intentional, peaceful, and "resting under the trees" reminds me of wilderness camping, one of my happiest recreations, and contentedly falling asleep in my small tent.

But honestly, is it possible to plan our own condition at the time of death? And even if a good death is what everyone wants, how do we go about making such an event possible? What insurance policy guarantees such an ending?

I don't feel at all happy about the idea of assisted suicide. But then, I've never been in a place where that has had to be considered. "Do not resuscitate" along with palliative care and relief from pain seems adequate, and while I hope that God knows best when I should die, I do trust my family and friends to make decisions when I cannot.

Jerry Hawthorne has died—renowned New Testament Greek scholar and dear friend from way back in Wheaton days. Clark

Pinnock, controversial theologian who once brought his class from McMaster University to a lecture of mine, has also died. Donald Bloesch, legendary scholar and writer, has died. Stacy, my friend from church. The crowd is gathering on the other side of the barrier.

John Wilson's review of *Long for This World*, by biologist Jonathan Weiner, quotes this: "We are always dying, and always reborn. And that is living. Our bodies are not finished products but works in progress, works continually being dismantled and repaired, rebuilt and restored, destroyed and healed at every moment in the act of living."[2] Wilson comments: "As we age, the balance gradually shifts: more is being dismantled than is being repaired. Why is that inevitable? Can anything be done about it?"[3]

Ah, yes. That's the unanswered question. I find this theme underlying much writing and discussion today. After all, the struggle with mortality is as old as the human race, though for years it was deemed unseemly or morbid to mention it. Did we think our silence and denial would banish it?

All the scientific efforts to extend the span of life fail to address the question: *unless we know life to be meaningful, why?* These renowned and fruitful lives are being snuffed out. They extended the boundaries of wisdom and knowledge and benefited their generation. Will their contribution count for nothing?

I guess it's come to this—I am searching, aching for the vestiges of what I was, while acknowledging the futility of such inspection. What I was as a young, eager, uninformed but curious and intelligent woman is somehow being buried. The decline has begun.

⁓

At the housewarming party for Greg and Suzanne one night, I felt in two minds about the kind of care and concern with which I was treated—someone finding me a comfortable chair, comments about how "fabulous" I looked (*and why not?*), concern about my drive home from Seattle to Bellingham in the heavy rain, friends finding my shoes from the cluster left at the front door, and general sweetness and compassion wafting my way. This is all very reassuring and heartwarming, but it made me want to stand up and say, "Why are you treating me like a fragile old lady? Please, listen. If I can be a forecaster you may understand this transition more clearly."

I've always wanted to be seen as someone at the heart of the action, at the center of things, not relegated to the margins because of perceived gender or weakness or weariness, an innovator, a strong-minded, action-oriented woman. I'm sometimes confused by these two perceptions competing inside me.

*Engine*

*For so long it has done its secret work,*
*my faithful heart—a fist-sized knot*
*of muscle closing and opening,*
*clenching and pulsing. Its names are Patience*
*and Perseverance. Its other name is Mortality.*
*What can a heart do but keep pumping?*
*Sometimes it jumps, misses a beat, races,*
*feels uncertain of itself for a few seconds*
*then pushes the blood to throb in my throat.*
*The doctor gave me a pill for that,*
*but I don't ever hope to have a heart*
*that doesn't leap with astonishments*
*too big to contain, like fireworks.*[4]

I hope someday to be juvenated.

One of the consequences of aging is the feeling of no longer being totally in the loop. I strenuously react to that by getting overinvolved in ongoing relationships and responsibilities, but realize the impossibility of really keeping up with the ever-increasing rapidity of culture change. The forward momentum of "progress" is dismaying, as it often seems to lack any component of reflection and deliberation.

⁓

The human vocabulary is constantly evolving, especially in the arena of technological innovation. John and I have the International Scrabble Dictionary for our evening games, and it includes words that weren't even invented ten years ago, including all the scurrilous ones. It's no longer cool to say "Cool!" or "Awesome!" For a while people were exclaiming "Wicked!" to express astonishment or delight, but that's now become a bit passé. "Kickass" and "Sweet" are common parlance, though not mine, and my friend Mark suggested I use the expression, "That's the bomb!" How long will those last? Not only do such expressions sound weird coming from my mouth, they make my kids roll their eyes.

And now I hear that the venerable *Oxford English Dictionary* will no longer be printed. The list of words has grown too long; to print or own a set of the new version is beyond the publisher's or purchaser's financial reach.

I love discovering the origins of words; what will I do without the *OED*, my favorite compendium of etymological instruction? Madeleine L'Engle and I spent endless hours speculating about the origins and evolution of words. I was thunderstruck to realize that *astonishment* actually reflects the shock of thunder. And that *cataract*'s two meanings—deterioration of the eye's lens and a powerful waterfall—both reflect the idea of "breaking down."

And now, both are beginning to apply to me.

# 9

# Learning to Breathe

*What utter bliss it is,* at the end of a long, busy day, to climb into bed, head sinking into my down pillow, under my down comforter, body deliciously horizontal on the foam mattress covered by silky sheets.

Now, if only I could put my mind to sleep.

I focus, as I have learned to do, on a mental scene. I zero in on a locker room, and my own locker, with a key in the metal door. The key keeps the contents locked away and prevents my thoughts from entering. If I can mentally focus on that key, my mind usually gives up and relaxes after a few minutes.

Another trick is to "go inside myself," to achieve an utter stillness, focusing my closed eyes on the insides of my eyelids, I feel my entire body as a part of my mind that is giving in to entire relaxation. My head, neck, torso, limbs, all joined and whole. Integrated. This stills my soul as well.

Lying there, my body is composed, with my hands crossed on my chest, the way it might be in a coffin at a funeral home. I am at rest. I remember a little poem, maybe a song, from my childhood, in which I was taught to ask my heavenly Father, "Teach me to dread / The grave as little as my bed." I remember asking my mother, "Is that true? Is a grave as little as my bed?" getting the whole syntax wrong, but the principle right.

But now, *comfort* is exactly the word to apply to my bed-cover, soft, warm. It feels like a reward, yet anything I've accomplished during the day is because I have health and strength and shelter and resources; I am gratefully fortunate, more so than the majority of this planet's inhabitants. So I appreciate my pillow, my comforter. My chilled body under this little wigwam generates a bit of heat that in turn warms up the sheets and reflects back onto me.

Rest is my reward after work. I have on my bedroom wall an exquisite piece of art by Erica Grimm, composed of steel, gold leaf and waxy encaustic. It is titled *Rest* and shows a young woman crouching, evidently taking a break after a strenuous run. When I look at it, I remember how heavenly it is, at the end of a long, cold, busy day, to relax, to take my reward.

I am at rest and delighted to let the day go. Like an athlete for whom training and relaxation are both vital.

～

Thanks be to God for massage! What a gift for both body and soul. Even the silence is healing, with the typical background of soothing pan flute music.

Yet a quiet conversation is happening between the hands of Sharon, my masseuse, and my body, the body of the client. (What cold, mechanical words for the relationship.) All the senses are alerted, then calmed. There's safety in it, in spite of the vulnerability of nakedness, giving one's body with complete trust to someone who is skilled and confident for manipulation and loving care in setting to rights what has been strained or stressed or damaged.

～

A fruitful morning, clearing my desk of leftover correspondence, doing laundry, knitting my granddaughter Ella's sweater (stripes of pink, blue, green, magenta and tan) and hoping she likes it. Trying out a new recipe for scalloped potatoes. Why does a series of tasks completed contribute so mightily to my feeling of well-being and worthwhileness? (Indolence results in the opposite—a guilt about the probability that once again I have failed to justify my existence.)

Comfort and relaxation come from work accomplished. The comfort that comes when a poem I'm writing has "found itself," or of having composed a Christmas poem once again, finding the right image to accompany it, getting it printed, writing greetings to friends from the list in my computer, to buying the stamps to mail the envelopes, to giving them over to the postal service after I walk to my mailbox down the road with the view of our lake and an eagle circling, blue and white above and green foothills all around. I lift the little red flag to alert the mailman. Contentment!

So at the end of the day I'm often contentedly in bed, but perhaps still wistful about a guest I welcomed in our church workroom during our alms ministry that morning, who lives on the street, whose bed is a cement sidewalk in a nook of a building, whose only cover in a biting wind may be a ragged blanket. *Wistful,* the word, meaning quietly attentive and seasoned with a touch of melancholy. A word Jesus used, in disappointment at being misunderstood: "Wist ye not that I must be about my Father's business?" (Luke 2:49 KJV). Didn't you know? How could you not understand?

And I do know, I wist, and am torn and conflicted and grateful and warm and regretful and relaxed and secure and longing for something better for my fellow human beings.

*Later.* Even today at prayer with Deb and Lydia, the three of us could only sit in silence together, beseeching, calling for God's help for the friends whose lives are falling apart and the universe where we feel of little use. Except to love one another, hoping that the love spreads beyond us.

And what of my bed in the future, with soft white satin pillows in a protective casket—how comfortable is that likely to be? The family and friends may feel better seeing their loved one tenderly cosseted and cared for, saying good-bye while calming music plays through the bland atmosphere of a funeral parlor. But the reality is that what still waits is the welcoming bed of earth from which there is no rising except of the immortal soul and some kind of heavenly body.

✍

All the most recently received Christmas cards have been sitting for months on the enormous brass tray that my parents bought in Morocco nearly a hundred years ago, waiting for my sorting and reviewing.

I hate to discard them. Today I went through about fifty of them, slowly, savoring all the love and friendship concentrated on those pieces of colored paper.

*Later.* The card sorting is done. So many beautiful representations of Mother and Child. Snow scenes. Candles. Robins. Holly. Camels. Angels. Family photos. The patient brass tray, after being a receptacle for months, is now back to being its brilliant self. This afternoon I polished it with Brasso and vigor, and it sits again like a sun in our living room.

✍

Every year, every month, every day I am a spy for sightings of the stunning, the unusual.

Last year in Santa Fe, New Mexico, I photographed a sphinx moth on a lavender bush, its long proboscis like a fine wire probing the blossoms, darting from shaft to purple shaft, quick as scissors. At first I thought it was a hummingbird, it was that large, with wings in a blur of flight and hover. Later I learned that though this moth is an insect and the hummer a bird, they are related. Their DNA is similar, as is their mode of flight and feeding. Remarkable! Just as all of us in the human family, diverse as we are, are connected . . .

Found a poem in the "Poetry" folder on my PC that had disappeared from my memory. It called out to me. I tweaked it a bit, titled it "Collection, Recollection" and sent it off to John Wilson at *Books & Culture*. He wrote back immediately, planning to print it! This makes me disproportionately happy! But how long will I be able to do this sort of thing, to write and send and be received, almost like a reflex?

Jennie posted on Facebook a photo of a salmon swimming upstream to spawn in a local Bellingham creek. She saw it while hiking and snapped it on her cell phone camera. The salmon was huge and tattered, and she said four tries were required before it cleared the rock slide, in the end "throwing itself" through the air to clear its obstacle.

I know that salmon die right after spawning. This is their final effort, and it reminded me of the intimate connection between new life and old death. I'm feeling buoyant with the idea that dying is part of birthing, with new life building on and taking the place of the old.

Today, dramatic lenticular clouds in an amazing sky. You can almost see the wind carving them, shaping them into flattened, lead-colored ovals, so you know there's a kind of ferocity going on in the spatial weather above. The forecast is for rain, but right now the wide straps of dark clouds are interleaved with brilliant blue and gold ribbons. The contrasts in the heavens leave me almost breathless.

Last night our church choir rehearsed the Pergolesi "Magnificat" at church. It's a wonderful, complex, glorious, fast-moving work, but because I was away when the choir first started working on it, I've had a hard time getting my part into my head. We had an alto sectional session midweek that really helped. Getting the Latin text to fit with the notes is the biggest challenge. But now I can't stop it from taking over my brain while I do laundry, write postcards, thaw fish for dinner. *Magnificat in anima mea Dominum.* Inspired choral music like this reminds me that music makes a great sustaining theme throughout Scripture, and that being in a choir brings us together in community and joins us with all the singers of the Bible in a way that is truly celebratory.

"Make a joyful noise" indeed. My voice may crack and my bones ache, but song is the voice of the Holy Spirit in me, as well as words and writing. They lift me beyond myself.

Yay! Garrison Keillor read one of my poems on *The Writers' Almanac* this week. This is the fourth time. I feel like we're becoming old buddies. Turns out it's a poem called "December." I loved hearing his gravelly voice on the podcast. The poem is about the silence of snow, and the heightened sense of hearing a snow shovel at work, all other sounds being dampened, something that Keillor and Lake Woebegon surely know a lot about.

~

I love driving in Bellingham in the spring. In spite of the chilly weather, all the fruit trees are "springing," singing themselves into being in magnificent displays of pink and white—apricot, plum, apple, peach, cherry—undiscouraged by the darkly looming clouds today. Soon each twig will display its bridal bouquet grown for this spring wedding. I know this from years of observation! Next, they'll grow so full and heavy with blossoms they'll be ready to throw their bouquets to the crowd, and I'll be watching for the petals to drop like wedding confetti, filling the gutters and swirling over sidewalks with their largesse.

In alms ministry today, we were able to scatter a few petals of heavenly largesse to ten of our Bellingham street people with a little of the generosity we ourselves have been blessed with. They are so grateful to be able to look us in the eye, tell us their stories, and receive a pledge for a gift, a hug, and then a prayer for God's loving help to go with them. I go away from a morning like this full of my own heart's gratitude and blessing.

~

On my drive up to Tsawwassen today to see Barb, my spiritual director, I and my Prius at a zippy 70 mph happily basked in some bright sunshine for a change. The sky above was crystal blue, and a swirl of cloud arced in the shape of a giant white wing. I felt covered and protected. And Barb, as always, helped me untangle a cluster of the issues I keep having to deal with. Like what to do about impatience and inner criticism of others, burning within me even if it's not expressed.

⁓

Bev has just had a birthday, her eighty-first. She will be leading a time of reflection on aging and mortality later this month at church. She is also writing her reflections as she goes, much as I am. Fortunately there's no sense of competition in this. Our lives and writing will inevitability reflect much that is different and much that is similar.

As we do most Mondays, Bev and the other four in our prayer group met here this morning. I'm surprised and delighted that though some of us in the group differ in our understandings of spirituality, faith and life, we can still learn so much from each other. It is mysterious how, though we come together from lives that are often very different, our experiences mirror each other's, with responses that are diverse but enlightening.

We learn together, sitting in my study with the sun coming in brief bursts through the windows, and our conversational sharing is in itself our prayer for each other, knowing as we do that God is with every snatch of conversation, every silly story or joke, every confession of struggle, every tidbit of encouragement. We are at all different stages of life, yet we feel bonded at the bone, knitted together.

⁓

Mother's Day Sunday, and a celebration of the role of my maternal life that proves to be more satisfying and blessed, and closer to my heart, than writing or art or friendship or even marriage. The work and longing of a lifetime, almost, have been invested in my children—the beings who had their start like seeds in my own body, who have bloomed and flourished, who overcame barriers and difficulties caused by my parental inexperience and ignorance, who grew as I grew, who now have lives of significance, who are learning along with their own offspring, much as I did but in a far more swiftly changing world.

So there were pleasurable moments as I heard from them all individually. Sweet messages in cards from Marian and Kris. A reservation at a local spa for a ninety-minute massage from Jeff. From Johnny and Christa in Thailand: "Mom, You da mom, Mom."

And flowers—yellow daisies and Queen Anne's lace from Robin. Queen Anne's lace is a favorite flower for us both. She and I remember her wedding to Mark, on an island in an Illinois forest preserve, when her wedding bouquet was made of those white lacy flowerets, exploding like fireworks. I hope to use those delicate flowers as objects to write about when I talk about poetry at an elementary school next week.

⁂

Last week a busload of thirty from our church took the three-hour trip down to Tacoma and the Tacoma Dome to hear Archbishop Desmond Tutu deliver what was being advertised as his last public address.

In that enormous space, along with a crowd of over fifteen thousand fairly raucous youth, we witnessed a show that included a Puyallup Indian drum band, acrobats, choral groups, gospel singers, rap singers, break dancers and politicians—our Washington State governor and others.

Until the climax, when this little unpretentious man in a dark suit and purple shirt and clerical collar came to the microphone.

His smile enveloped the crowd. He spoke with immense humility and authenticity about God, who created our universe without our help, who had helped him in the battle against apartheid, who had rooted in him the concept and creation of the Truth and Reconciliation Commission that brought an end to much of the violence and bitterness, who now asks us individually to share God's love by each giving our negligible loaves and fish to be multiplied in the world. I felt a rising warmth and joy within myself.

❧

Today at alms ministry we had a revealing cross-section of humanity as our guests. Really gifted, competent, articulate businesspeople who had been laid off because of our recession, a young mother living with her children in a van, two victims of domestic violence, and sobbing, destitute, desperate people, some who could barely put together a sentence in English. We give each one a small olivewood cross to remind them that God's caring love goes with them. In one way or another, I think each was encouraged.

For me the vital part of the whole process of hearing their stories and offering resources is to remind them of the heavenly Father's love for them, to hug them and pray for each one. Then their tears are in response to love, not just a sign of desperation.

# 10

# The View from the Slope

*My latest exercise in paying attention* is to notice the houses I pass, driving along Lakeway into town probably twice a day. It means I'm seeing homes I've never distinguished before as individual, just themselves. I take note of the paint color on the front doors, the sidings, the roof angles, the landscaping. I wonder about the family that lives in each. Are they happy? What relational drama might their home contain? I try to direct this intentional look at the people on the sidewalk as well—taking nothing for granted. Why is he slouching? Is she in pain? How extraordinary it must feel to have that pink and purple hair!

Why do I struggle to find meaning in everything I see, and everything that happens? I'm wishing I could learn to simply attend to what is there, and then to open myself to being seen and enlightened by God. Might this become the place of balance and peacefulness?

Because I am a poet, I've been involved all my life in paying attention to the details of what I see, hear, smell, taste, feel, and then clothing those observations in words. Someone has called our eyes, ears, noses, tongues and skin the windows of the soul. Exactly. And if I am cut off from those windows, my recognitions of reality are diminished and I am deprived of illumination. I have friends whose vision is impaired. They compensate by becoming more acutely aware of what they hear, smell, feel, taste.

I've often quoted Annie Dillard on being a witness to existence: "We are here to notice each thing so each thing gets noticed and Creation need not play to an empty house." This is a
dictum that has taken root in my consciousness.

I'm drawn to the verb *attend*. Drawing on my four years of
high school Latin, I realize that the root word suggests a leaning
*toward* what my senses and my mind reveal to me. Even a leaning
*into* those particulars so that I am surrounded, suffused, with
sense impressions that then are received and recorded and am-
plified by my brain.

Awareness. Attention. Attentiveness. In a *Daily Beast* editorial
Tina Brown complains that our "attention is being fractured" by
the clutter of information that almost blinds us and blows us
away in its storm. Rather than clarifying, it confuses. Clear
purpose and discernment are clouded.

Intuition leads to attention, which leads to perception. To be
attentive means that the mind is always at the ready. And the
eyes, ears, senses, soul—all our separate selves joined in one to
observe and try to absorb and gain enlightenment.

⁕

"You will do well to be attentive to this [the prophetic message
from the eyewitnesses of God's glory on the Mountain of Trans-
figuration, including Peter, the letter writer] as to a lamp shining
in a dark place, until the day dawns and the morning star rises
in your hearts" (2 Peter 1:19). This is one of the most vivid
metaphors in Scripture for me.

A spark of light in a dark home before electricity, when all that
was available was an oval clay lamp, small as a potato, hollow
but filled with oil, with a hole at one end in which to insert a

wick and light it—how vital it was for keeping the room's occupants not only illuminated but oriented. In an impenetrable dark it's all too easy to imagine the worst, to stumble against an unseen object and lose track of one's place in space. This is the message that I hear: "Be attentive to the message of good news, and let it light up your life. Attend! God is there if our eyes are open to him. Come to attention!"

Several Bible versions use the term "the Majestic Glory" to describe the speaker at the baptism of Jesus by John. Remarkable that Scripture links this ineffable, overpowering light to the tiny glint of an oil lamp in a dark room!

I attend as well to more mundane paths to enlightenment—even a page that I'm reading, where often a word jumps out at me, almost pleading to be used in a new context. A word like *buttery*, or *cerulean*, or *porcelain*. And the serendipity! How often, when I'm preparing a speech or an essay, I find the corroborating or expanding information in whatever journal I'm reading, or in the morning newspaper.

❧

Today—the first day of fall. Though both are equinoxial, I count spring, with its sense of leaping up and release from cold ("spring forward"), as fall's opposite. And fall—we fall back into it as well as falling back into standard time. *Autumn* has a derivation that suggests ripening. Perhaps that should be my ambition—to hope my life will ripen into sometime edible and nourishing and pleasing to look at.

My senses are so drawn to the foliage today. I almost melt in worship of the tender shades of rose and gold and russet and lavender. The leaves are especially brilliant this fall. The leaves on the dogwood trees are like flames of fire in my front yard.

When driving I keep pulling over to the curb and photographing
the ground overlaid with gold leaf, literally. I keep my little
point-and-shoot camera at the ready in my purse for this sort of
spontaneous activity. I notice that the maples and liquidambars
seem to drop their leaves almost deliberately, patterning the
grass in a way that is too unstudied to be replicated by a human
being arranging things for a well-composed photograph. Their
lovely, loose exactness needs no forethought. No amount of re-
arranging them, placing them aesthetically to make a better
photo, can achieve this natural "effect."

I want to be a leaf. I'm even ready to fall, but not this fall.

Some evenings at the Glen Workshop in Santa Fe, Greg hosts
"after parties," when faculty and friends can get together up the
hill at his apartment. After a while I nearly always find myself
out on the balcony with the guys smoking cigars. The other Greg
supplies me generously with cigarillos. The little ceremony
when he lights one for me and I suck air in to get the tobacco
fibers glowing, and then breathe out a lovely plume of smoke,
introduces me to a different world of male companionship. A
little light flirting may happen. Liquor and laughter flourish, and
the conversations are the result of all the good creative work that
has been happening earlier in the day, full of bawdy humor and
shared wisdom.

There are a lot of intense, intelligent people here. Intensity
often seems to go with great giftedness. The level of intellectual
literary conversation is high, and one feels an obligation to
always be intelligent or mordantly witty!

So it's a relief to return to my little monastic cell of a dorm
room and close the door and silently talk to my laptop or the

darkness. The window is open. I smell the tang of the pine trees outside. A silky shawl of air flows in from the night. I'm energized by friends, yet right now I am peopled out, hungry for the quiet of aloneness. So many thoughts to sort out, like the fibers in a tangled tassel.

A free day in Santa Fe. On the drive I took to the Bandelier National Monument, I couldn't escape the overpowering sense of time and its work on the aged New Mexican landscape. So many layers of sedimentation, like fossilized club sandwiches, with contrasting strata laid down eons ago at odd angles. Some of the rocks, the remnants of volcanic tuff, are pitted with holes like Swiss cheese, natural dwelling places that the ancient peoples took advantage of for warmth or refuge. Strange, uplifted red rocks that rise from the bluffs, icons like ancient animals scrubbed to their elemental shapes by erosion. And we travelers, tiny sparks, shivering stars in the long night of history, casually cruising along highways that follow the tracks of those ancients, themselves momentary, sparks in that same long darkness.

Our little flashing eyes absorb these evidences and move on with barely a thought except to comment on the strangeness of the ancient landscape. We are small animals whose uniqueness comes from mobility and the ability to reflect on our own insignificance. Again and again I'm reminded of my own brevity, my peripheral value to the universe. We think the human race has power to change the world, but we have little compared to the volcanic eruptions and the mighty heaves of a hidden giant who can lift a mountain like a chunk of cheese in the hand.

And the sky! The clouds, such colossal, melodramatic structures of moisture carved by wind and rising draughts of air. Here in New Mexico they start around midday as small and innocent wisps, or shapes like skullcaps on the hills, or develop into cirrus, before they begin to gain authority in brilliant white cumuli and nimbi. Never the same configurations, they seem endlessly creative; the shadings of white and gray and the billowing contours of their ascent, like the sails of great ships, astound me as they build to blackness until their fingers of dark rain swoop down in shafts and drown the land, blotting out the shapes of the mountains with angled gray veils (Georgia O'Keeffe painted it so vividly). All the little dry gullies respond with liquid gurgles, and then suddenly the sun strikes through and gilds everything—the sagebrush achieves a neon green, the cottonwood trees breathe fire.

### Thunder and then

*Thunder and then the rain comes and the*
*prairie that has been baked dry and the*
*shriveled grass and the ground that has*
*thirsted all summer open like mouths as*
*the wet arrives at first in whispers and*
*then in sheets of silver arrows that tear the*
*air and join like the clapping of hands to*
*a downfall that makes splashes in the dirt*
*and grows to pools that shine in the silver light*
*and the dry creeks with their stones begin to*
*thank God for sending water for their need*
*so that there is praise in the rushing streams*
*and the trees also raise praise with their leaves*
*flashing and now wind like a fist takes hold of the*
*house and shakes it and us and it seems that*
*all the world is drowning in the delight of deluge.*[1]

And later that night, the enormous clarity of dark, the resolute whiteness of stars and the whole universe holding its breath. I'm exhausted from prolonged astonishment.

Yet this is so good for the human soul. *This* reduces us to what we are—mere insects or grains of sand in the scope of our ancient earth, with only a morsel of intelligence and comprehension, yet capable of wonder and a kind of ecstasy at such phenomena. How to retain this bliss, this euphoria? It evaporates almost as soon as it has overwhelmed us.

In our arrogance, we like to think in terms of control and invention and power. But we are at the mercy of elements above and beyond us that can flick us and our belongings into oblivion in a tornado of violence beyond our control. And we are conscious of the uncertainty of life.

Listening in on a conference call, a "town meeting" hosted by AARP throughout the state of Washington, I heard two Johns Hopkins physician-educators discussing ways for seniors to stimulate and retain attention and cognitive ability. According to the phone operator, there were over eight thousand people throughout our state who were listening in and asking questions. This is the generation to which I belong, so I was interested, though actually I learned nothing very new.

I did notice that most of the questions were from women, many with voices husky with old age. One woman in the queue of callers was brought into the conversation and asked by the host, "Helen, what was your question?" She answered, "Oh, sorry. I've forgotten!"

Another incident yesterday, as I listened to Terry Gross on NPR while driving into town. The topic was "mindfulness." And

I remembered an email from a retiring minister who was hoping to start retreats on the theme of "soulfulness" (which takes the thought a little deeper). My almost instant reaction to these words was a wish for further definition. But however you want to define *mind* or *soul* or *spirit*, the implication is that this is a kind of mental conditioning, a sharpening of our mental capacity to be aware.

I'm coming to believe that such awareness is not simply a brain function. Though the brain is involved in recognition and perception, it is through our senses that we become aware. I often drive familiar roads almost automatically, my mind on other things. This is often a time when my thinking develops along new lines, fresh observations, and I often grab a key word out of the air to help me remember for later. A word like *clouds*, or a phrase like *rags of snow*.

I'm convinced of the need for mindfulness while I'm driving— an even greater need as I get older—but it's because I have eyes to see the road conditions, road signs, traffic lights and the trajectories of other cars, as well as ears to hear sirens and engine noises or feel the thump, thump when I have a flat tire.

⁓

My tendency is to analyze experience, and then to analyze my analysis. It's an internal, intellectual focus on myself that could easily end up as morbid introspection. This effectively closes the door to the sense of Presence, for which I long.

Regarding the risks of self-assessment, self-awareness, I recently read *Copenhagen,* an intriguing play by Michael Frayn about the unexplained visit that physicist Werner Heisenberg made to Niels Bohr in Denmark during World War II. In this book I learned something about observation of subatomic particles and what has been called "the uncertainty principle."

The principle learned, articulated by Erwin Schrödinger in the context of the impossibility of quantitative observation of electrons, also applies to our own souls, our minds, our motives. It is almost impossible for us to examine ourselves dispassionately, objectively.

In the book's epilogue, in which Frayn describes the research that went into the writing of the play, he remarks, "One's thoughts and intentions, perhaps one's own most of all, remain shifting and elusive. There is not one single thought or intention of any sort that can ever be precisely established." Self-consciousness creeps in whenever we try to assess our own state of mind; inevitably it muddies our conclusions.

Ideas, images, words, tunes circle the brain like a scatter of leaves in a gust of wind. Things shift and slip and reshape themselves during any mental process of self-examination. In the very effort of introspection we put our own thoughts and ideas to flight by our attempt to analyze them.

It is all too easy to deceive oneself. Most of us would admit to thoroughly mixed motivations for the projects that are of greatest importance to us. We may try to be candid with ourselves, but the search for "the self within the self" may easily slip past reality into either morbid introspection or self-absorption, unless it ends up striking through to our heart of hearts and discovers God there all along.

I need an Eye, an Ear beyond myself. Someone who does "pay attention" and is utterly aware. Honest, friendly critique has its benefits, but in the end no human seeing or listening will do. My most intimate friends, my colleagues, my spouse, even my therapist or spiritual mentor may be deceived or make wrong assumptions about my inner life, no matter how candid I have been about my thoughts and feelings.

It's not that we lack the skills and abilities to do what we do. Human beings have been granted the abilities to be competent and creative, and we often are. I'm not an academic or a scholar, but I yearn to learn as I go. Like a comet, I trail behind me a plume of work well or poorly done, including writing that seems to me to justify its existence as a reflection of the real. But I must ask, what is its eternal value? Is it done to God's glory and the benefit of the human race?

From time to time I've been asked by interviewers what boils down to the following question: "How did you develop your career as a writer?" I feel rueful as I think back and try to find an answer. The truth is I've never intentionally built "a career." The word itself sounds so self-assertive, so narcissistically confident, so marketable! And it's never felt like that at all. Writing has always happened for me naturally, without the hope of future glory or acclaim. If I thought something was worth writing about, I wrote it. If it found an audience, that was wonderful. Poetry has never attained a lot of popularity in the general readership, and even less among the Christian faithful.

And yet it has always felt that this was what I was supposed to do. Determined by whom? Well, by whatever or whoever dropped the gift into me. And I have always believed what St. Paul wrote to his young colleague Timothy, "Rekindle the gift of God that is within you" (2 Timothy 1:6). If a gift is there, it carries a responsibility. The metaphor that has always come to mind for me when reading Paul's directive is a coal in a heap of glowing embers. To keep it alive and hot, it needs to be stirred up, agitated, allowing oxygen to reach it and feed the heat. And if that coal is in a community of other hot cinders, what joyful flames can leap up!

So, a career? Nothing so intentional and forward-looking occurred to me. My life was and is full of children and grand-children, and when I was first married, right after college gradu-ation, freelance editing work filled the empty spaces. We were poor, in a one-bedroom apartment with our first two babies, and poetry had no way of changing that. Poems came in the cracks between other things, like having four kids in six years and making my husband's meager salary, gained in Christian min-istry, last. And then came our fifth baby, ten years later, to dem-onstrate that I was still fertile!

Then, back in the early '70s, Harold' and I started a publishing company. When my first book of poems, *Listen to the Green,* was published (it seemed the obvious thing for us to do) I heard some grumbling aimed at Harold: "Well, he *has to* publish her stuff. He's married to her!" The implication was that it was a vanity project. But in truth I was just deeply grateful to have a publisher husband who valued my poetry and believed it worthy of publication. For many years we continued to publish poetry as well as literary biographies. That was our mandate, to bring into print imaginative, creative work. At the time, few other faith-based publishers felt this imperative. After Harold's death in 1986, I continued this work, eventually selling our publishing house to WaterBrook Press.

*　　　　　　* ⋙

I'm becoming conscious that when I invite God into every task, seek his wisdom, trust him for help when I get stuck, the work itself becomes a sacrament. The imminent and the tran-scendent join hands, as in the life of Brother Lawrence, who made a practice of noticing and affirming God's presence in his most menial tasks, such as washing pots and pans and peeling potatoes.

My prayer today and into the future is this:

*O LORD, you have searched me and known me.*
*You know when I sit down and when I rise up;*
  *you discern my thoughts from far away.*
*You search out my path and my lying down,*
  *and are acquainted with all my ways.*
*Even before a word is on my tongue,*
  *O LORD, you know it completely. . . .*
*Search me, O God, and know my heart;*
  *test me and know my thoughts.*
*See if there is any wicked way in me,*
  *and lead me in the way everlasting. (Psalm 139:1-4, 23-24)*

&#x1F3B5;

Lately I've been bemused at the sight of glowing laptops being held at odd angles in the dark (during a candlelit party, or late at night in a coffee shop) while their owners work away on this awkward rectangle. The term *laptop* seems flawed; it rarely fits a lap. For all its competent, sleek design it is such an angular, manufactured object.

I gave John a painting for our twentieth anniversary—a pastel landscape from Lynn Wilson, a gifted artist friend at church. As we hung it on the wall above our fireplace, with its burnished gold frame, I began to wonder about the human obsession with other rectangles—objects with four corners—frames, tables, windows, houses, TV screens, books and the pages inside, envelopes, bricks, city blocks, city-planning grids and so on. Is this just a habit that we haven't learned to break? Does it make life easier and more efficient to always be—square? Is a rectangle or cube the most economical use of space or containment, whether two- or three-dimensional? In my simple life, rulers rule merely for the measurement of surfaces. (I do remember protractors and compasses from math classes.) A circle feels more universal, as a natural form (think planets and raindrops), and hexagons (as in honey-combs and Petoskey stones) cluster together neatly so as not to take up much space. I'm thinking of writing a poem that might start like this:

> *A square is not a natural shape,*
> *inelegant, unlike the curve*
> *of wave or drip or egg or grape.*
> *Its sharpness calls me to escape*
> *rigidity. I'd rather gape*
> *at flow and pearl and flight and swerve . . .*

I'm no mathematician or spatial geometer or engineer, so these queries are only little trial balloons of thought sent into the troposphere, and merely examples of my quest for answers, often the spur for greater curiosity, one hopes.

Time is a tide that keeps moving, edging, inching up the beach, stroking it, lapping its small wetness in ripples over the pebbles, the shells, the kelp and the trillion grains of sand, each like a second of time passing, each with its own unfathomable beauty that deserves its own occasion to be seen for itself, but is overcome and submerged too fast for inspection.

Flannery O'Connor once said, "The writer should never be ashamed of staring. There is nothing that does not require his attention." I remember sitting on a beach on Sanibel Island, its shores famous for their vast variety of shells. I was able to remain happily sitting in one place for hours, seeing and sorting and saving every tiny shell that caught my eye. Multicolored, shaped according to their species, they glinted with shade and shine, especially when touched with the first waves of the incoming tide. My pockets filled up. But then I had to move as the water advanced and the wind rose and a storm came in, driving me back up the beach. There were so many other shells I'd had no chance to admire and glory in.

Am I talking about aging? There's so much still to be learned, to love, to celebrate, to grieve, and the waves keep advancing.

I wonder about interactions in my brain. Yesterday I had a flashing impression of a pattern in red and black that seemed to come and go in my imagination and of which I took passing note. I remember noting its existence but not what the pattern was like.

So one thought seemed to perceive another thought, observing it without pasting it into memory. Like particles in the Large Hadron Collider that leave infinitesimal traces of their passage, my neurons are like friends in an idle conversation not worth recording but leaving a trace of the communication. This passes understanding! What else is buried in there?

# 11

# Lightening the Load

*Snow settled gently* all this morning—about four inches worth. At first fine and fast and almost invisible, and then dropping in huge, slow flakes that look like tufts of congealed feathers.

*Later.* Now the cedar branches are beautifully bowed over, obedient to the weather and the white. The glorious clematis that sent out its pink-and-purple blossoms all summer has finally succumbed to the cold and hangs, brown and shriveled and limp, from its vine. I felt a pang, as if this must be what I have to look forward to, as if my final years will chill me until life is gone.

The roads are tricky with ice and packed snow. Some ditches are blotted with cars awkwardly askew after a skid, abandoned by their owners for the tow trucks to deal with. Crashes and accidents are being reported all over Washington. People have been hurt, or have died suddenly, violently, before they were ready for such an abrupt transition. Change happens.

"Acute and upright" is how the latest *New Yorker* describes a ninety-five-year-old writer who has just published her first book. Hers seems like an aspiration of active old age that is worthy of serious consideration.

What will I be like at ninety-five? Will I ever *be* ninety-five? And is it OK to long for longevity? Right away, I know my answer: *Only if I am of sound mind.* I know the body is already folding itself, getting ready to be put away in somebody's closet. This morning the hair on the right side of my head was ironed flat with sleep and my face was seamed with little valleys. Sometimes my visage comes to life again in the shower and an anointing of moisturizer, but I'm aware of what a losing game this is.

I'm tempted to ask, *Why bother?* The birthdays in my eighties and nineties are coming at me like a series of blizzards in this wintertime of life. Spring will come to the hills and valleys, but how and where will I join its green newness of soul and body?

December, and time to begin sending Christmas cards, the annual effort to stay in touch. I have my new Advent poem written and its accompanying illustration already designed and printed as a greeting, and today I began to go through my computer list for addresses to inscribe on the matching envelopes. This register identifies my tribe of friends and relations far and near.

The older you get, and if you did the usual procreative things earlier in your life, the larger your clan. In spite of all my trial-and-error parenting, my grandchildren are getting married and fruitfully producing their own offspring, and my Christmas gift list increases along with the tribe! My laundry room, with its wide flat shelf for folding shirts and other garments, is a scene of chaos and creativity with ribbons and boxes and glitter and multicolored tissue and wrapping paper and gift tags overflowing the entire room, so that actual laundry becomes a mere secondary activity.

So today I'm off to the post office to unburden myself, the back of my car loaded with parcels. Being the matriarch gives one a sense of gratification (I've done my part by adding to the gene pool and producing healthy specimens with diverse gifts and abilities). I'm part of the ongoing human enterprise. And now I must live with the resulting responsibilities and burdens and delights.

※

Names. Addresses. I'm distressed as I survey the list and make corrections. People have married, divorced, moved and died. Again and again I have to delete a name—a longtime friend or the spouse of a friend. I can so easily change a mailing address, but when I hit "delete" for a name—Jerry, Georgia, Carl, Rusty, Royal, Edward, Gil—it feels as though I am jettisoning that person into unreality, almost canceling his or her existence with a keystroke, leaving a blank where there had been a valued human being of long acquaintance.

Likewise, I acknowledge that the structure of my life, the scaffolding built over many years, is falling away, being dismantled, disassembled. My memories are still sharp and vivid, but when I go, so will those recollections of mine. And history never accounts for all the details.

※

Fierce prewinter winds. As I drove home from church, my car was being pushed sideways by the gusts like the snow, almost horizontally. And coming round a corner, I saw a huge inflatable Santa lying on his belly, his jolliness flattened by the storm, his head buried in a bush. The mighty has fallen.

A new poem came today, a memory of a California weekend
years ago:

### The Promise

*"Follow exactly the path that the* Lord *your God has
commanded you, . . . that you may live long in
the land that you are to possess." Deuteronomy 5:33*

*In Mendocino County we stopped for
a wine-tasting. The hills were radiant with
light and fruit. We bought a dry white and
after lunch at the vineyard café
we walked the rows of vines held up
on their supports like old men on crutches.*

*Business was light that day. Want to see
something crazy? the owner asked. We clambered
down to a cave a hundred feet under the slope,
and felt in the earthy dark a tangle of root fibers.
A flashlight gleamed, and the beards
of the ancients lit up like live wires.*[1]

This promise of Yahweh in Deuteronomy seems to me to
speak of the blessings of old age, of hanging on through drought
and flood, poverty and plenty, of an attitude of courageous persistence as our roots deepen and spread. It speaks of being
grounded(!), so that one's roots can continually be sucking up
vital moisture and nutrients. Of "possessing" our land the way
roots possess the soil and prevent erosion. There's such fulfillment in this metaphor, as it includes the grapes on the hillside
above ripening and yielding their juicy, winy crops, season by
season. Wine is a symbol of joy and shared companionable cel-

ebration in Scripture. I'm thankful to apply such a metaphor to my own existence.

~

Jesus matured into adulthood but never experienced getting old in his earthly life. Does he understand what it feels like to be me? Knowing the universe by heart, having invented it, he never needed to ask my kind of existential questions (though he often taught his friends by asking *them* probing questions). But perhaps his all-knowingness includes his understanding of all my uncertainties, all my inquiries.

~

December 29, my birthday—eighty-four today. There were more than eighty Facebook birthday greetings for me, as well as a number of cards through the mail. Quite encouraging and heartwarming. *They haven't forgotten me!* I so long to be present in people's hearts, as they are in mine.

I don't feel any older than yesterday, but in my morning mirror I wondered if my face looked thinner. Am I shrinking? Is it morbid for me to look for signs of age and to keep checking on myself at the center of my life? Is it too self-involved and self-absorbed?

I think it's only by admitting my feelings and experiencing them to the full that I gain an understanding of what aging is all about. And I find that I'm entering more fully into others' responses and experiences as they age. Three people in our church died last week—reminders of the reality of mortality.

I got a new iPhone 4 from John for Christmas and birthday. (Since the two events come so close together, I'm never sure which gift is for which event, but it was a generous, welcome gift.) So I am learning some basic apps and actually made a couple of easy phone calls this morning and scheduled a forty-thousand-mile car checkup for the Prius on this very smart phone. My family is taking me out for dinner tonight. I feel so relaxed and pleased about that; no worries about what to prepare for the evening meal, tonight at least. A lovely kind of freedom and anticipation.

~

The new wisdom, as reported in *Newsweek* this week, is that people in their sixties and seventies are the "young old" and those in their eighties and nineties are known as the "old old." Saw this gem of wisdom on Facebook, attributed to Neale Donald Walsch: "Life begins at the end of your comfort zone."

These later decades are not quite our best years. And hope that scientific breakthroughs will extend our richly useful lives still waits for fulfillment. But as Susan Jacoby, in her book *Never Say Die*, comments, hope is not a plan. Faith, hope and mystery cluster within us like the Three Graces, though charity still outshines them all!

At eighty-four I am barely into the "*old* old" category. And I like to think that I am still useful and flourishing in most of the ways that matter to my family and to me. I am still coherent. The words that I need in my writing come without much effort. The ideas form and take language almost instantaneously as I ponder. My relationships are warm and mutual. My body still functions. Mostly.

In the new yoga class we signed up for, I'm flexible enough to achieve the poses with a little coaching and a careful nudge from the teacher here and there. I am, however, a bit skeptical about the instructions to "allow your eyes to sink down into your skull" and "visualize your third eye." Or "broaden the space between your eyebrows." My logical mind tells me, *Rubbish!* Though I want to allow this process to work some health in me, I know a bit too much about human physiology, and such ideas run counter to this knowledge.

*⁣⁣⁣⁣⁣⁣⁣⁣⁣*

We're following up on our major decision—to downsize. We adore our present home, designed and built for us by daughter Robin (an interior designer) and her skilled builder husband Mark fourteen years ago. With a southwestern theme, with curved arches and nooks and Navajo rugs and Mexican *saltillo* tiled floors, it was planned for guests and gatherings. But we're trying now to employ foresight by buying a vacant lot closer to downtown Bellingham and, more importantly, just five minutes' drive from Robin and Mark, who will construct the new, smaller place and keep an eye on us as feebleness and incompetence inevitably overtake us.

I write this jauntily. It seems distant and unreal.

*⁣⁣⁣⁣⁣⁣⁣⁣⁣*

John and I met with Robin and Mark some nights later to start discussions about our new house, which we are all looking forward to their building for us. The restaurant in which we met was dramatically dark, with only pinpoints of light flickering from table candles, and after a fruitful planning time, with lists made and preferences outlined, we left to go back to their house for ice cream. On the way out I didn't see a step down and fell headlong, dramatically. The embarrassment was worse than the fall, with kind men at neighboring tables scrambling under their chairs for my purse and its contents—lipsticks, keys, tissues, et cetera. "Are you all right?" "Here, let me help you."

I got to my feet, gathered my wits and kept reassuring people around me: "Yes, thank you so much. I'm fine. It's OK. Sorry to bother you. Yes, not to worry." I wonder, does having white hair and the melodrama of falling qualify one for extra concern? Once more I felt that my age placed me in a special category in which I'm considered incompetent and helpless.

Or am I simply in denial?

~

Aha, the whole concept of downsizing—in length of life, in the need/want continuum, in living space—is beginning to get real. I went through several drawers and shelves yesterday and decided I could dispense with nearly all of the contents. Thank God the church rummage sale is coming up soon! And thank God for Hope House, the local source of help and household goods for needy people. We are filling large bags and boxes with items still useful but redundant. It's like lightening the backpack!

This comes in conjunction with my reading, in manuscript, of Paula Huston's wonderful *Simplifying the Soul,* which arrived at this opportune time.

Some conundrums remain, such as what to do with family treasures, many passed down from earlier generations. My mother labeled many of her charming and valuable possessions for us, her children, individually, before she died, a practice I hope to emulate.

Over these many years I've traveled widely, saving up air miles for trips abroad or responding to invitations to conferences overseas. I've never been wealthy, but such opportunities for journeying have exposed me to the riches of other cultures. There are the objects with sentimental associations from such trips: "I bought this plate in Portugal on a trip with Harold." "This etching came from the retreat in Iona with Madeleine L'Engle."

I have collections of pebbles plucked from beaches wherever I've traveled. I carry plastic bags for collection purposes on beach walks; I simply cannot resist doing this and once ended up with a backpack of stones so heavy I could barely climb the cliff up from the shore with it. The stones come home with me and rest in ceramic bowls and bottles around the house, reminding me of their original settings.

I have a superb group of Petoskey stones, those fossilized hexagonal corals from Michigan, gathered with my friend Carolyn when we sailed the Great Lakes together in the '90s. And other smooth stones, rounded from wrestling with waves and rubbing against their pebbly kindred. Pebbles from beaches on our nearby Lummi Island, many with intrusions of quartz that bisect them like lines of light. I have a glass bottle of pink and white quartz stones gathered on Long Island Sound, and sea glass in glorious greens and blues and ambers from the Northern California coast. Each of them, in its moment, was a treasure not to be ignored but picked up and stowed in a backpack for its trip home. The way God chooses and cherishes each of us, each of us his special one. I wonder, *Am I a stone or a bit of driftwood for God?*

What to do with all my hand-thrown pottery, much of it signed on the bottom by the potter? And the beautiful New Mexican pottery, baked underground with dung to turn it a distinctive black? The Navajo rugs, each with a photo of its weaver pasted on the back? The Barry Moser prints of winged creatures, including angels? A Roman glass bottle from an antiquities shop in Old Jerusalem?

When the children were young we spent many summers on

Cape Cod, replete with old barns and boutiques. In my study I have a window shelf reserved for a row of old glass bottles collected from New England antique shops or washed up on sandy beaches. Some of them, narrow, tall, small-mouthed, held medicine, Castoria (a purgative). Or root beer. The squat ones contained ink. Each is unique. There are more than thirty of them, large and small, aqua and white, clouded with iridescence. When the sun shines through them they glisten in their pale, translucent beauty. Remainders from the collection urge the desire to own and enjoy and preserve and remember.

And there's the glorious goose-necked bottle of antique pressed blue-green glass, given to me by Josie B. She had to downsize too as she grew older, and years ago relinquished this treasure, admitting as she handed it to me, "I want you to have this, but know that this really hurts!"

My corner cabinet displays hand-painted bone china cake plates with gold-leaf rims brought home from England by Harold after World War II. China too beautiful and fragile to use except on grand occasions.

The Georgian silver coffee and tea set left me by my Aunt Lucy, going back several generations.

Many original artworks purchased from the artists—sources of continuing aesthetic pleasure.

But perhaps letting go of the garden, which we have so diligently designed and planted and weeded and loved as each plant flourishes and blooms, will be the hardest. We can't take the dogwoods, or the lavender, or the rhododendrons and peonies with us, but they will be there for the new owners, the ones who occupy our house. We hope they love it all and make it their own.

But OK, I need to remember, "Where your treasure is, there will your heart be also" (Matthew 6:21). My greatest treasures are my family, my heart-friends. They're not going away.

So, discernment. What do I really need? What is worthy of being held on to? Where does my heart reside? What is my basis for value?

~

Today, in our weekly parish prayers at St. Paul's, when several of us meet to pray for both parish and personal needs, I asked for my partners to pray for wisdom for John and me in this process of divestment. (Perhaps its opposite, *investment*, could lead to the development of the inner life?) Diane, a long-time fellow prayer, suggested this sequence concerning discernment, based on what Jesus said, quoting from the Torah (Deuteronomy 6:5): "You shall love the Lord your God with all your *heart,* and with all your *soul,* and with all your *mind,* and with all your *strength*" (Mark 12:30, emphasis added). In this series, loving God with all one's strength flows from loving him with all one's heart and one's soul and mind, springing from each previous surge of love for God. So in the process of discernment, our decisions should all flow from the ultimate source, our strong heart love for the living God. And that shines a different light on everything!

~

Big day today! John and I met with Robin, Mark and Grant, the house designer who fourteen years ago drew up the plans for our present house. It's exciting and astonishing to pin down some imaginative ideas, aspirations that have been simply moving around as pictures in our brains, and watch as they are translated into words and gradually take shape in a list of requirements and hopes, and from there find a shape from computer image to blueprint paper that will eventually take

physical, three-dimensional form real enough to live in. Each
of the five of us contributed relevant information. And now we
have a plan!

※

Three days of unremitting rain.

The weather forecast predicted "sun breaks" today. And
against all expectation we actually had one! It lasted all of a
minute and a half.

Rain is the predictable price of living in this, one of the most
greenly beautiful parts of the world. Thus the inscription on the
moss-covered standing stone in our front yard, engraved with
another old, brief poem of mine: "Planting seeds / inevitably
changes / my feelings / about rain." Though we are at the top of
a long hill, rain is pooling on the driveway, under the trellis,
spilling into the gutters. Our ravine resounds with the roar, the
white noise, the fierce hush of the stream below my study
window. We'll leave all this behind when we move.

Mark tells me the ground is still too soggy to begin clearing away
the blackberries on our expectant vacant lot: "It would just make a
muddy mess." Season and weather dictate so many of our decisions.

※

A fascinating little family drama played out before our eyes
this morning. Deb and I were waiting in my kitchen for our
other prayer group members to gather when a slight movement
caught our eyes through the window. The wooden birdhouse
Mark made for us last year began to sway violently from its hook
under the balcony, and from the small round hole in its side a
dark blob began to emerge.

We watched intently. Finally we realized that it wasn't a bird but rather a squirrel mother with a baby squirrel clinging around her neck. We could see his tiny pink hands hanging on for dear life. Even with this burden she clambered easily to the top of the birdhouse, leaped over to the deck post and down onto the deck railing, and scampered along it, finally flinging herself and her infant onto a cedar branch and down into the ravine, disappearing into the ferny shadows.

When we went out on the deck to look more closely at the birdhouse, we noticed that the entrance hole had tooth marks around its edges, enlarging the hole so that a creature somewhat larger than a bird could squeeze in and out. What do you call a baby squirrel, a kitten? a pup? Google won't tell me. I'm naming this new one Squirt, and wishing him long life and happiness.

I suspect that mother love was at work this morning, as it is throughout the animal world. Did she realize that her baby would soon grow too big to get out? Or was she simply eager to usher him or her into the wider world with its pleasures and dangers? Maybe she was upsizing rather than downsizing. Perhaps to the squirrel that first view of sky and woods and space feels like what I may feel when transitioned, released into the larger life.

⁓

The idea of downsizing keeps bringing with it for John and me an overwhelming realization, the requirement to sort and sift through all our belongings, combined over twenty-one years ago after our separate widowhood, and accumulated over our two lifetimes. Some inherited treasures, many works of art acquired firsthand from their artists, all the books, the rugs (my Turkish living-room rug was purchased many years ago with my first poetry royalties), the silverware and dishes, the furniture, all require the discipline of simplification. What do we really need? And is retaining a bit of beauty in our living environment reprehensible? I guess we could live in a barren barn or a sparsely furnished apartment, but beauty and art feed our spirits and reflect something of Grace in our lives.

My son Johnny Shaw, after a brief stay with us over Christmas, just moved back to his medical work in Thailand with two suitcases. On a scale of divestiture larger than ours, he had gone through most of this with Christa last summer as they moved out of their home here in Bellingham.

Their ultimate questions, which we continue to ponder, are, what do we need, and how do we decide? In a talk at his church, Johnny evaluated this process of *sifting belongings* together with *combing through life options*, especially for someone committed to serving God, comparing himself and Christa to a pair of suitcases packed with certain gifts and abilities and life experiences —he with his tropical medicine and public health degrees, she with her life of teaching and counseling young people—that are being opened up and made available to others.

I really like that image, even though I'm a ratty old suitcase worn at the seams with one of its wheels damaged so that it bumps as I pull it down some aisle in some jetway. In this chronicle of my later life I'm spilling stuff out of my luggage, like a trail of underwear bursting out as I go through security and get x-rayed and felt up and vulnerable without my shoes. No flight risk here.

I also love that I can learn from my children.

⁂

Lately we've been meeting with a loan officer at our local bank as she has been processing some of the documents to do with our new purchase of land. She looks uncannily like Miss Piggy of Muppets fame, with the same heavily mascaraed eyes, extended upturned lashes, tipped-up porcine nose, and cute little mouth between chubby cheeks. The likeness is so remarkable that I expected her to answer our questions with "Who, moi?"

Later I mentioned this likeness to John, and now both of us think of her as "Miss Piggy at the Bank," which is clearly so unfair! I'm terribly afraid I may someday thank her for her services by remarking as we leave, "Thanks for your help, Miss Piggy."

Lord, have mercy.

Today we've finally become the proud owners of our own sloping quarter-acre blackberry patch that simply yearns to be built on. It has been sitting there, waiting for us, for at least forty years.

We closed the deal in the presence of our friendly realtor Barry, who has tenderly shepherded us through the ungainly and finally concluded process of negotiations of price, requests for site plans, loans, lines of credit, permits, legal documents to be signed and dated, and multiple handshakes at our good fortune in actually finding good, available land close to the heart of rapidly expanding Bellingham.

Now, when the blackberries on our lot ripen this coming summer, they will tilt their small dark globes toward the setting sun unknowing, not expecting that their little lives will soon face total eradication.

Yesterday, a step toward sprucing up our present house for the ultimate offering on the real estate market. We called on Jack, my handsome grandson who works for Mark, his dad, at Schramer Construction. He got to work with his pressure washer for most of the day, cleaning up the outside of our house, hosing away grime, green slime, spiderwebs, decapitated moths, wasp nests, leaves and twigs and needles in the gutters, and generally leaving the whole outside gleaming. It's the exterior version of spring cleaning, that annual routine in which the insides of the house are restored to pristine orderliness.

And we need to get even deeper inner work done. "Create in me a clean heart, O God, and put a new and right spirit within me" (Psalm 51:10). Spruce me up, even if it takes power washing!

~

"Search me, O God, and know my heart." I'm finding that whenever I begin the inner journey of prayer, my request that God would investigate my hidden heart clears the way and opens up my own thoughts to me with greater clarity. God's inquiries and my own subterranean searchings join together in a profound desire for oneness with him, and results in a willingness to search out and pursue his way for me.

During Lent a couple of years ago, my forty-day reflections were on my human tendency to seek recognition as a writer, to lust for acknowledgment, approbation and significance, and to realize that if that became my consuming desire, it would be toxic. I wrote about it in an essay, "Ambition," in *Radix* magazine (*Radix* 35, no. 4). I continue to deal with that issue, which doesn't want to go away. But then, in 2011, I was seeking guidance for my discipline in the coming weeks.

Ahead of time that year I hadn't felt particularly engaged with the whole idea of Lenten self-examination, fasting and preparation for entering the meaning of Jesus' life and death. Until as a lector at our Ash Wednesday service, I read to the congregation the passage from Isaiah about God's view of the legalistic "fasts" of his people ("Look, you serve your own interest on your fast day, and oppress all your workers") and the prophet's desire for a new understanding of the compassion for others that God wants to see in us: "Is not this the fast that I choose, to loose the bonds of injustice . . . to share your bread with the hungry . . . and satisfy the needs of the afflicted" (Isaiah 58:3, 6-7, 10).

This was indeed a moment of self-examination, and I felt it borne in to me that impatience is one of my prevailing faults, especially in relation to my long-suffering spouse. I became convinced that part of the generosity God delights in is my gift of patience to people in my life. Here's the promise given to the generous: "*Then* your light shall rise in the darkness. . . . You shall be like a watered garden, like a spring of water, whose waters never fail" (Isaiah 58:10-11, emphasis added).

During the liturgy our whole congregation then read together Psalm 51 with those same penetrating words. "Create in me a new heart and renew a right spirit within me."

This internal perception, this conviction, this sense of openness to God for his correction is then emphasized by the external marking of ashes on our foreheads—the burnt remnants of last year's Palm Sunday palms recycled for sacramental use. So now, for a day, we wear a symbol of death and a reminder of the priest's words, spoken as he made a rude, cross-shaped smudge on the skin of each of us lined up at the altar rail. I still feel the imprint of that human thumb, and those human words echo in my mind, "Remember that you are dust, and to dust you shall return."

As if I didn't know that.

But I also know that the awareness needs to sink in deeper. Somewhere, hidden in that ash that will become a kind of fertilizer for new growth, is the promise of Easter, of rising, as the buds of my crocuses are pushing up even now through the sodden ground. "For as in Adam all die, even so in Christ shall all be made alive!" (1 Corinthians 15:22 KJV).

So there's a significant difference between New Year's resolutions and Lenten disciplines. The first tend to be in one's own best interest. The others are for God. Already my determination to curb my impatience is being tested, which shows me how badly it is needed! It makes me realize how bossy and critical I tend to be about annoyances and trivialities that are truly trivial.

# 12

# Liftoff!

*On the car radio* on the way to church we often listen to a
sacred music program offered Sunday mornings on NPR. Today
it was something Spanish, then something from Latin America.
It seemed uproarious, exuberant, not a bit tired of the festivity
of the Easter season.

It struck me how nothing can really be as expressive as music,
with drums, strings, wind instruments, keyboards, timpani,
other exotics such as Indian instruments, as well as the amazing
reach and timbre of the human voice.

It's as if no matter how gifted we are with spoken or written
words, we need another way to enthuse or grieve or give voice
to what we're feeling emotionally. Think of the wild applause
that follows a bravura solo performance at a concert. Think of
belting out our enthusiasm when our candidate is elected or our
team wins the trophy. Think of wailing at loss. Think of how
the dirges of bagpipes seem particularly fitting at funerals. And
the "Hallelujah Chorus" captures exactly what we feel about the
incarnation of God in Jesus.

Just as walking is inadequate when we're happy enough to
need to skip or run or dance, so speaking may feel not emphatic
enough to express our emotion. Even though a poem can reach
into our souls from the silence of the page and turn us inside

out, we also crave the vibrations of musical instruments and of our own vocal cords that express our sentiments uniquely.

Music brings such an expansion of the soul. It is often a spiritual exercise, as Hildegard of Bingen believed. With its power to lift the spirit, it energizes the whole body. In singing, especially some of the ancient masses and chorales, as well as traditional hymns, earth joins heaven in the medium of our human vocal cords.

I don't have a solo voice, but I learned to read music early on when I was taking piano lessons at the Toronto Conservatory.

But being in a choir is exhilarating. Even when my voice cracks or fails to quite reach the higher registers (I'm an alto), I feel something magical, miraculous, is going on. There's something about singing with others, as I do with our church choir, that forms a unique community. Choir practice with Wade, our gifted music director, is a high point in my week.

In C. S. Lewis's *The Four Loves* he describes the kind of friendship that involves working together, shoulder to shoulder, toward a common goal. Our common purpose as a choir is threefold: to sing well enough to feel confident about it, to please our choirmaster and to praise God.

How much of life was created as a balancing act. We breathe in oxygen to revitalize our circulatory system and in turn vent carbon dioxide to refresh the green things on the earth's surface. Male complements female, winter wakes into spring, daylight balances nightly darkness, moon alternates with sun, activity is balanced by rest, community is enriched by times of solitude.

The *via negativa* of asceticism in single-minded service to God is balanced by the *via affirmativa* of jubilation and gusto. Gravity and levity achieve a kind of complementarity, as do lethargy and energy. The prolonged silences of monastic meditative prayer are countered by contemporary praise songs and the rhythms and foot-tapping that accompany trumpets, guitars, drums, cymbals, and joyful noises and "all kinds of music" as called for in the book of Daniel. Contrast is a vital tool in reaching an understanding of our being. Ours is a chiaroscuro existence in which light shows up the shadows and vice versa, and it takes all varieties of human being to provide the perfect mix.

Even among circles of Christian faith, I want to celebrate the rich diversity of expressions of our life in God; it speaks of divine generosity that matches need with gift and inclination.

Whether you're a Baptist, a Presbyterian or a Pentecostal worshiper, God loves you and your varied styles of worship and proclamation. With Plymouth Brethren (my foundational group), you celebrate "the simplicity that is in Christ," and your love of Scripture is praiseworthy. Orthodox? Conservative? Progressive? Liberal? Each of those characteristics has its own flavor and outlook that may be honored by God, who looks at the heart.

I love Episcopal and Lutheran liturgies and history, and Catholics have been stabilized through the centuries by their honoring of the Magisterium—the teaching authority of the church. Our faith is strengthened, enriched and sustained within these wide-ranging understandings of life in God.

I remember hearing a preacher say: "The kingdom of God is not a matter of buying and selling, but of giving and receiving." Our openheartedness with each other furthers the purposes of our God of love, who calls us to celebrate our faith together.

I don't believe in "just believing" for the sake of being able to say I have faith. Belief and faith and trust need an object, not necessarily something we can explain or describe in detail, but something or someone of substance, attested to by other believers. And tested in the light of our own experience.

# 13

# Mountain Pilgrimage

*. . . and miles to go before I sleep.*

ROBERT FROST

Lately I've noticed that traveling tests me to the limit. The extra-early rising to catch a plane, the laborious hauling of luggage onto the aircraft to avoid paying an extra fee (John dislikes checking baggage, which is OK for him, but juggling a heavily packed suitcase and my weighty briefcase and getting them into the overhead bin and under the seat tax my meager strength).

But it's the preparation for travel and change that gets me excited. I enjoy planning, thinking ahead, deciding: "Small or large suitcase?" Then collecting and packing things together, arranging for the mail to be held, the paper canceled, the houseplants watered. I anticipate the freshness of another landscape, the interesting people to connect with, the photo ops and the challenge of, perhaps, a foreign language. Even the books that I have postponed reading, keeping them for the trip.

I am pretty orderly in my packing. I try for color coordination in clothing, as well as weather wearability. It's my old bringing-order-out-of-chaos motivation. I realize that the words *order* and *ordinary* come from the same root. Perhaps the need for orderly packing is a desire to have some predictability, some ordinariness, to take some familiarity along with me to a strange place, to have my recognizable possessions with me though everything else will be surprising and different and exciting.

Yet when the time comes to lock up the house and drive to the airport, I realize I'm leaving my conveniences behind—my own bed, kitchen, study, books. My reasonably regular schedule.

Sitting on a plane with barely room to cross my legs, with schedule delays for weather or "mechanical problems," with uncertainty as we circle and circle over a city before landing in fog and we miss our connections, long layovers in some run-of-the-mill airport, all this sucks much of the joy out of travel. "Should I stay or should I go?" becomes a familiar refrain.

*≈*

The word *peregrine* is related to *pilgrim,* a wanderer; certain falcons are named "peregrine." For me it's a reminder that no human being has a permanent home. Except, for the Christian, a destination called heaven.

I've done some almost endless trips, one from Queenstown, South Africa (after visiting my Johnny and Christa), to Johannesburg to the Cape Verde Islands to Amsterdam to New York to Salt Lake City to Seattle, and then a slow bus ride for the hundred miles north to Bellingham. On another trip the bus was delayed by a snowstorm, and I didn't get to Bellingham until 2:30 a.m. and barely found my parked car under the thick snowdrifts.

This is not a complaint; it was worth every millisecond of

fatigue to have the enchanting visual memories of being together with Johnny and Christa. But I wonder, as age takes its
toll, how much more energetic travel I can do without wilting,
or cancelling.

(I should mention that I have three Johns in my immediate
family: brother, husband and son. John is a lovely name, and I
don't regret their each having it. But clarification is often needed
to tell a story about one of them. When they're all here in my
house together, I just have to yell, "John," and three good men
will jump to attention! So for the purposes of this telling, my
husband is John and my son is Johnny.)

*≋*

On another trip many years ago, after traveling from Nepal to
Bangkok, with a day-long visit with a pastor friend in Hong
Kong, followed by a flight across the Pacific to Seattle, I reached
home in Bellingham to find my little forest cabin flooded out, all
the pipes burst from the freezing cold, and rather than being the
restful, reassuring place I'd hoped for, my home was an emergency that had to be dealt with.

And I'm reminded, again and again, of the long trip toward
my ultimate destination. How inconvenient is that likely to be?
I wonder, are my travel experiences prescient? How will this life
journey end? Does global and personal disaster lie ahead? Is the
trip to a far country worth the effort?

*≋*

When traveling in Wales (Welsh is my family heritage on my
maternal grandmother's side) I used to be enchanted by the pre-
fixes to place names—Pol and Tre and Pen and Ben. Now I ask:

What's the point of gaining this knowledge? How will I ever use it? Do I have enough life left to apply it? How would such lexicographical knowledge make me, or the human race, any better? Or is the fun of it, the entertainment of the strange and delightful, excuse enough?

P.S. Reflection on sleeping arrangements in B&Bs in the UK: I often feel like the hot dog in a bun: thick white duvet covering me, white-sheeted box mattress under me, with me between— the meat in the middle.

I looked in the mirror yesterday and was pleasantly shocked. Maybe a good night of sleep had eased some of the wrinkles, but I looked and felt really well. (Forgive this note of female self-congratulation; I comment on my appearance not as a matter of vanity, more as a kind of reassurance that the speed of decline has maybe slowed a bit.) This, in spite of the trauma of our trip back from Europe—six legs from Venice back to Bellingham under the influence of a cough, bronchitis and a potent cough syrup that made the entire journey seem like an extended bad dream.

John and I had spent a week gliding down the Danube on a river cruise. It was a pre-celebration of our twenty-year marriage, and one of the rare trips we've done for pure pleasure. And I *was* able to glimpse the charming and intriguing landscapes of Germany, Austria, Slovakia and Hungary while peering from the porthole, though in a narco-syrup-induced daze. Bronchitis is not the best of traveling companions, and coughing away the nights resulted in days of exhaustion. The castles, village churches, grand cathedrals and autumn foliage seemed like a series of missed opportunities for enrichment. And then, the four days in wonderful Venice before the six-leg trip home!

## Traveling

*It was a dream. At first it was*
*a good dream. I was floating down*
*the Danube when Budapest drifted by,*
*all cathedrals and spectral lights.*

*Vienna, then things turned bad.*
*Through the porthole I coughed my greetings*
*at Melk and the wine country.*

*The boat's elevator went only halfway up.*
*Or halfway down, depending on one's*
*degree of optimism. Downstream,*
*toxic sludge had turned the blue river red.*

*In Venice the vaporettos weaved left,*
*right, to S. Stae, San Marcuola.*
*The Grand Canal was a snake.*
*The Guggenheim, full of colorful*
*abstractions. My drink of choice became*
*an addictive cough syrup in Italian.*

*Coming home we were in a vast airport*
*with no signs to anywhere and*
*the self-check-in machines not working.*
*The clerk at Information left for lunch*
*as soon as she saw us.*
*There were rumors of strikes.*

*Paris, and armed guards moved in.*
*"Back, back," they motioned, without*
*saying why, until everyone was gone.*
*This was alarming.*

*I was hunting for my boarding pass,*
*but nowhere. An eternity later I got a new one*
*but the number was wrong and so*
*was I. Security patted me down, and down.*
*They found nothing, like me.*

*The Jetway turned, and turned*
*to a small round hole in the side of a plane.*
*We began a flight around the world*
*but only got halfway. Sometime after that*
*I leaned my way onto a bus*
*and the driver said kindly*
*only two hundred twenty-five stops*
*to go. Then it was later.*

~

Years ago, when I was visiting Johnny and Christa when they were still working in South Africa. Jeff, two years younger than Johnny, and his then girlfriend Donna, now his wife, came with us as we drove in a *bakkie* (truck) from Queenstown to the Kruger National Park, the boys in the front, driving, and we three women in the back seat. We anticipated the opportunity to view the elephants, lions, panthers, elands, alligators and other wildlife in their own wild territory. Johnny and Jeff had the map, and they would frequently bend their heads over it, discussing, over several days of traveling, the best routes to take.

Years before this trip, I'd visited the Masai Mara game reserve in Kenya. This enormous wildlife park gave us marvelous opportunities to view the vast distances of the Rift Valley. I was with a group of Bible translators, and together we saw elephants mating, a pride of lions sleeping after feasting on the carcass of an antelope. Giraffes, zebras, monkeys were freely inhabiting the grasslands and trees. In the pop-up van roof we could safely view it all—as if we were in a cage of safety and the animals in Eden-like freedom!

Until the seasonal rains came, just before we were due to return to Nairobi. The dirt roads and trails were immediately transformed into mud like heavy glue up to our hubcaps, forcing us to get out and push. We arrived at last, back at our city hotel, exhausted and streaked with the dark clay.

≋

I love maps. Always have. In my late teens I often accompanied my dad, a popular conference speaker after he retired from being a missionary surgeon, as we traveled from Toronto into the United States and out to the East Coast and New England. He drove and I was his navigator. Dad and I would pore over the maps to figure out the most appealing routes. He had an intense interest in the history of the places we visited, a fascination that communicated itself to me. We took some of the back roads—more interesting than the freeways—to make our way to various churches and summer conference grounds where Dad was a welcome and well-loved speaker.

So on our South African trek with my kids, I got pretty frustrated at the way the boys in the front seat of the truck were hogging the map, with me trying to get in on their route decisions as I hung over their shoulders from the back seat.

I love exploring beyond the lines, including the routes on a road map. (Now instead of paper maps I use a GPS, perched on my dashboard.) Of course, a map is only a kind of label, like the ones on bottles of Tylenol that say "Directions." Maps are not the real territory itself; they give limited information, even the large-scale ones, and they have to be translated into a larger kind of reality.

I once did a solo road trip (as a kind of silent retreat) from the San Francisco Bay area to Arizona and New Mexico, and on the way home saw on the map what I thought was a shortcut between two main highways. It turned into a red dirt road that wound up steep escarpments without protection along the edges, which dropped off precipitously to canyon floors. Mile after mile, hour after hour it continued, with no road signs, no fences, no signs of human habitation, no campgrounds, just endless chaparral. The sun was setting and I began to get anxious, thinking I'd have to camp in the desert with coyotes howling around me all night.

I began to pray for some sign of humanity, and within a few minutes I came around the side of a mountain and there was a small B&B with a couple of tent sites, and two sweet elderly Christian women anxious to feed me and settle me in for the night. As I erected my tent I felt wonderfully comforted and calmed. Adventure is OK, especially when it finds what it's looking for!

≈

So, maps. Perhaps they are metaphors of progress towards a resting place, an ultimate goal. I used to teach courses in journal keeping as a means to self-awareness and God-awareness. One of the exercises I suggested was this: "See your life as a landscape. Describe its contours and challenges, and think of yourself as traveling toward a destination. What is it, what do you expect along the way, and how will you know when you get there?"

≈

The forward momentum of change seems to be accelerating, as evidenced by the speed of the modern news cycle and the blaring shallowness of much contemporary thought and conversation.

Atlanta airport on my way to Charleston, South Carolina, for a fiction workshop. Changing planes, I was descending an escalator with my two pieces of carry-on luggage, one perched on another, and they fell apart at the bottom of those steadily grinding stairs; in trying to pick them up I fell on top of them, hordes of passengers coming down behind me, piling onto me. Embarrassing. Humbling. I imagined the other travelers looking at me with pity and annoyance, thinking, *That old lady shouldn't be traveling alone.* A youngish man helped me up, realigned my bags and got me onto the electric train to the next gate. This was not one of my best moments.

At the marvelous Mills House Hotel, a historic landmark mansion where our group was staying in Charleston, all shining marble and elegance and efficiency, one event disturbed the serene surface of things.

At 2:30 a.m. a fire alarm sent us all, scores of guests, down the stairs and out onto the sidewalk in our night gear. It was 40 degrees F, chilly and windy, and we shivered in groups as we were surrounded by four immense fire engines along with cop cars with sirens and flashing lights. Interesting to see all the wealthy, sophisticated guests out in the night without their daytime faces on or their hair combed, or their jewelry!

A friend of mine in the crowd was panicky and trembling, not just from cold, and I was able to hug and reassure her. I think I'm good in a crisis, though this was not a serious one. (I used to dream of being a nurse in an ER, expecting to relish the drama and eager for the opportunity, as is my penchant, to bring some order out of human chaos and catastrophe.) As it turned out, the hotel fire was a small one in a laundry room, and once the smoke was cleared from the corridors we were allowed back in, to our elevators, rooms and beds.

Today, after returning from Charleston and the lovely seminar with Bret Lott, I'm feeling full of go and gumption, answering mail, paying bills, laundry, grocery shopping and more. It feels good!

The time with Bret and the others in the group was energizing, though I still don't feel called to write fiction. As Bret kept emphasizing, "No conflict, no story." The only conflict I'm feeling right now is the pressure of overactivity, yet everything I'm involved in feels good and right and fun and somehow worth talking and thinking about.

≈

November 29 was my dear Madeleine L'Engle's birthday. When she was living we kept track of each other's celebrations and often spent them together—mine just ten years and a month behind hers. My home office is studded with gifts from her: a crystal statue of Mary and Jesus, a prayer book and Bible combined in one enormous volume, leather-bound and stamped with my name on the front, a wood carving of angels, an evil-looking beaked gargoyle (she said the room was looking a bit too holy, with all the angel images!). I usually gave her earrings or books or furry hats for winter, for her daily walk to the cathedral for noonday prayer.

One year I asked what she wanted for a gift. "Go on a trip with me" was her immediate response, and we traveled together by car from Bellingham up into the Canadian Rockies, staying at some expensive resorts and making up for the extravagance by checking in to a couple of cheap B&Bs.

We also traveled around Scotland and Ireland with our mutual friend Barbara, inventing rowdy limericks as we drove. On the island of Iona, we spent meditative time in the ruined nunnery where Catholic sisters had been slaughtered by overzealous Protestants. This was in spring, and the bare hills and fields were dotted with yellow irises. The abbey looked out over the crystalline blue ocean. Sheep wandered everywhere, and the hills echoed with the earthy sound of grass being cropped. With its freedom and beauty it was a holy time.

～

December 17, and winter solstice is approaching—when the sun seems to stand still and wait for the baby's birth. And this time we're off to a cabin in the Sierra Nevada to spend time in the snow before Christmas with John's daughter Lisa and her family.

The incongruity in Reno Airport! Slot machines (I nearly wrote "clot machines") were clicking and clacking and whirring everywhere, intently crouched over by people with, presumably, nothing better to do, while Christmas carols—"It came upon a midnight clear, that glorious song of old," even "Silent Night"— tried to overpower the clatter of the greedy money machines.

*Later.* We're up near Donner Pass. As we trudge from the car along the driveway and into the cabin, the snow is falling thickly, while the tall ridge-pole pines sway like ancient dancers in the blasts of wind blowing so fiercely that it knocks huge clots of snow from their down-sloping branches, briefly blinding us and chilling our cheeks.

Together the next morning John and I go for a walk along the road below the cabin just to experience snow, its power to paralyze, its chill and purity, its simplicity and implacability.

The wind has died. The snowplows have worked all night, carving away the drifts from the road and leaving white cliffs six feet high, clean honed as if by a knife. Exquisite in its detail, everything is a black-and-white photograph but for slots of color in the cracks and crevices that had been opened by the plow in the packed snow cliffs. I photographed their deep, mystical blue—a kind of intense indigo-turquoise I remember from glaciers in Alaska, the result of light refracting in ice crystals under pressure.

One of the little gifts I have brought for Rachel, John's oldest granddaughter, is a beginner's knitting kit. Nikky, her younger sister, gets a potholder loom with colored string to weave. Each turns out to be just the right thing.

We work together on them most of the afternoon, sitting together in front of the fireplace and its blazing fire. Rachel catches on fast and completes about four inches of a scarf right away, without a single mistake.

For days now she's kept at it, and I feel a sweet kind of satisfaction at having helped her learn something she loves and will be able to enjoy for the rest of her life. She's eight and Nikky's six, and with me at eighty-four, we've connected happily in the middle over potholders and knitting needles!

Now I'm on to the sleeve of a green sweater I'm knitting for Wade, our church music director.

Hoping for all the simples of wilderness, for this holiday I've most anticipated a silence that might liquefy and inform my soul. But in this "wilderness" cabin there is a microwave, an oven, a refrigerator, a dishwasher, a wall phone, four iPhones, two laptops and baseboard electric heat. We're grateful for their convenience, of course. But as I see the snow mount against the windows I almost long for it to overpower technology and test our survival strategies.

But then I am invited to check my email on Ben's computer, and learn that *Books & Culture* has chosen my poetry collection

*Harvesting Fog* as one of its ten best books of the year, along with
the works of a bunch of theologians and other eminences. And
I am buoyed by the swiftness of imparted information.

⌘

Flights to and from Indianapolis for a family wedding the following spring confirmed my distaste for flying in winter. Mechanical difficulties are one thing (and we all want our machines
to work well when they are sustaining us at thirty-six thousand
feet). Fatigue of crew members is another (no sleep-deprived
pilots, please). But weather is uncontrollable. How can we
forgive it or make excuses for it?

In Minneapolis, my layover airport, a blizzard, at total white-
out level, delayed my flight back to Washington (due to repeated de-icing and snail speed along the runway before
takeoff). Missing my Seattle connection to Bellingham required
some quick, clear thinking if I was not to just book a hotel
room near the airport for the night. So I called the Airporter
Shuttle, reserved a seat and settled in for the two-and-a-half-
hour drive north to Bellingham. My checked luggage finally
made it by air yesterday.

I'm glad I can still manage this sort of thing on my own. I was
just congratulating myself for having found our Subaru among
the thousands in the local airport parking lot and driven home
in the sleet and the dark, when I stopped at our mailbox, hopped
out of the car to pick up the accumulated mail and fell flat on the
fiendishly black ice that covered our street. It was a nasty jolt,
humiliating, though in the dark no one saw me. There are purple
bruises on my right hip, my knee, my elbow. Nothing broke.

I was reminded that at my clinic the doctors always ask me,
"Have you had any falls lately?" Falls are a telling symptom of

aging, a portent of coming doom, and I have learned to confess my tumbles honestly, even while making excuses that always sound a little hollow. The rug was wrinkled. The ice was slick. I didn't see that curb until too late.

So I'm caught in that crack in my life's canyon floor when the inevitable is becoming all too possible and frequent. And one of these days something may indeed break.

I'm in Texas to speak at a university's annual honors program celebration and waiting in a hotel lobby for the department head to pick me up. Behind the hotel reception desk is a screen that proclaims a list of the hotel's amenities in a looping series of flashing colored signs, nearly all with multiple exclamation marks. "!!!All Day Breakfest!!!" "Late checkout! Lay in bed til noon!!!" "Exercice room. Its all URS!!!"

I have to look away from it; the misspellings and grammatical errors agitate me.

Am I too picky? Language is so important, to me and to our stories and to God. Should anything be done about this kind of careless slippage? Has education not informed our children about the value of this most fundamental of human activities? Has speed become the operative word, rather than accuracy? Does any of this really matter?

I suspect this kind of casual attitude to words is endemic in popular culture. Which is why I so applaud the efforts of literary journals like *Image* and *Books & Culture* and *Radix* to make compelling, well-put language attractive to wider and wider circles of readers.

I picked up an infection on the plane coming back from Dallas. It struck me down the way a tornado scatters the straw of an old scarecrow across a field. With John away in California, all week I've lain like a corpse in my bed, aching, weakened, feverish, miserable, and I'm struck with how lonely I can be in my sick body. No matter how much compassion, support, sympathy comes to me by phone or email, no one is able to feel just what I'm feeling. Our human understanding for each other is limited by our encapsulation in the discrete cells of our own individual beings.

While lying in bed with time to think in the ragged way that fever produces, I remembered lines and phrases from a couple of old poems of mine, about intimate human connections and the isolation of illness: "We have been seamed, / not grafted"[1] and "we are agnostic / in the face of dying."[2] At the time of that early writing, I'd been reading something by Flannery O'Connor who suffered a much more devastating disease than anything I've had to deal with. What she said was: "Sickness is a place . . . where there's no company, where nobody can follow."

This is one of the human predicaments Jesus came to reverse, in his own incarnation, enfleshment. My old poem continues, "Only [God]'s son, . . . / in bearing all our griefs / felt them firsthand . . . / in the messages of nails."

Strange how one's own thinking and writing echoes from the past to speak to one in the present. I think of Holy Week, when those ancient griefs and sufferings of the Word himself, the Logos, the Ultimate Communicator, is foremost in our minds, our readings, our music. "Help me, Lord, to enter into something of your own experience, as you have entered mine."

In this new week I feel as if I have risen from the dead. This time it was antibiotics that accomplished the miracle. This is a huge relief, as I must prepare to fly to Toronto tomorrow to participate in *Image's* board meeting with our new Canadian board members. A wonderful public event is planned in the Glenn Gould Studio, where I'll be reading poetry along with John Terpstra and joining him in a panel discussion about words.

Now I'm home again from Toronto, with mind and memory flooded by the events of this past long weekend, complicated and tiring, but all rich, all joyful. My soul and body have to catch up before I can feel at peace and begin again to enjoy the present. I want to be present in this present.

And yet with nothing but the small 2"×2" notebook in my purse, with a few words scribbled, how can I recount and record the events in sequence in a way that lets me move beyond?

After the meeting with all our Canadian board members, I attended another gathering, the Friday night "Aunt Invasion" with all my Canadian nieces and nephews and their vigorous offspring in one of their homes for hugging and photographs and a great barbecue. The men of the middle generation (my brother's sons, all vigorously halfway between youth and age) show the results of maturation and male pattern baldness. The women, my lovely nieces, welcomed me with embraces, their faces warm with affection and laughter. These people are my flesh and blood, and we'd been too long apart. I think they were grateful for a good excuse to be together.

Being away, even for four days, means an intense time of catching up. My desk is a young mountain range of paper. My email overwhelming. Phone messages. Other people's urgencies.

At a deep level, I know why this busyness, this movement, keeps happening. It's because I keep saying yes. And yes. And yes. Not wanting to miss anything. Not letting myself let go.

And then, phone conversations with Marian, Kris and Jeff set
the tone for the day, and give me courage and energy to start
whittling away . . .

~

Such a sense of joy and fulfillment today. Johnny is home from
Chiang Mai, Thailand. Christa will be joining him here in about
a week. My family will all be congregating on our West Coast
this coming month.

I picked my son up at Vancouver airport yesterday, an airport
that, like most of the great airports of the world, seems to re-
arrange and extend itself every time I'm there. Because it's designed around a wide curve, I find it hard to remember where
my car is parked, on which level, in Domestic or International,
facing north, or northwest, or west, or some unknown planetary
direction. As I park the car and head toward the terminal, I try
to take careful note of my route—down the blue-painted staircase
from the parking garage, across two roads, past the bus station,
through the automatic doors, past carousels of arriving baggage.
I find a woman at an Information booth and ask, "Which way to
International Arrivals?"

She gives me a series of complicated directions. It takes me
about fifteen minutes to walk, and ride elevators up, then down,
then up again, and along, and finally arrive at the point where
all the foreign travelers emerge from Customs and Immigration
with their bags to be identified by their loved ones.

The monitor tells me the Korean Air Flight 71 has "landed"
and then "arrived." But I know how long the lines are, and immigration followed by baggage claim processes can sometimes
seem endless, with carousels making their continuous circuits
like shining Mobius strips.

The anticipation mounts.

Finally there he is, lean and tall and brown, with two large suitcases and a backpack—most of his earthly necessities. Together we try to retrace my route back to the parking structure, and after some trial and error, we find the car and finally head south across the border to Bellingham. A great sense of rightness and relief floods us both.

# 14

# Incidents and Accidents

*A routine colonoscopy today.* As usual, I was mildly sedated but was awake enough to be fascinated seeing on the screen the images of my interior, that part of me that doesn't see daylight, that I have only rarely met before under similar circumstances, all pink and juicy and spiraling like the inside of a shell. No polyps were to be found, but my little diverticuli showed up, another symptom of the aging of the body. I tell them to shut up and not make trouble.

A new word is entering American conversation—*amortal,* its defining characteristic being "amortality." This is clearly not the same as immortality; rather, it is described as a stage of life during which the process of aging is being artificially slowed down with the ongoing use of substances like human growth hormone and testosterone.

"Amortality" is the enterprise of Dr. Jeffry Life(!), whose photograph showed up in the latest issue of *Time.* He promotes a program that he describes as "the world's largest age-management practice." At seventy, he's upright, with a buff, toned and tanned torso. But I look closer—his face is sagging and wrinkled, hairs protrude from his nose, much of his scalp is bald, and the veins in his arms and hands stand out like swollen rivers. His program, Cenegenics, in Las Vegas, purportedly allows for an extension of life and hence the practice of what sounds to me like a frenetic lifestyle—sports, partying, luxury travel, sex, food, "fun," et cetera, all in the name of health.

It's hardly worth mentioning that this will be the domain of the über-wealthy who can afford the drugs and treatments and live in the artificial communities designed for and devoted to the pursuit of pleasure and perpetual youth.

This sounds rather like desperation to me—incessant stimulation without true satisfaction. In this scenario one looks forward to a pleasure cruise to Samoa, or the excitement of intimacy with the attractive new man or woman in the community, or the installment of a new spa where one can be pampered and feel rejuvenated. For the moment.

But even in the moment of anticipation, at the heart of each little hors d'oeuvre of appetite, hides the awareness that this new experience will shortly be over and all one has to look forward to is the next, and the next, each a tad less satisfying in its failure to deal with the tedium and mindlessness of self-absorption.

When one becomes the focus of one's own existence, responsibility and care for others dwindle. Voltaire said that "no snowflake in an avalanche ever feels responsible."

No matter how much pleasure and energy you hope to squeeze out of some transitory stimulation, the question that still hovers over this program is this: unless one's life has meaning beyond one's own temporary pleasure and vigor, why struggle to extend it? Continued diversion from boredom is in itself boring in the end. Human death is inevitable despite any efforts at distraction and prolongation. One can only temporarily put off the decay of the body and the entry into the afterlife.

Today my world tipped over a bit, tilted about 30 degrees off
normal, flipping from theoretical to substantial and real and a
bit threatening. Last week, after days of low belly pain, I saw a
doctor at my clinic (not my usual doc, who wasn't in that day),
who ordered a scan.

In preparation I drank what is optimistically known as a "wild
berry smoothie," a bottle of barium contrast fluid, and some
hours later a second one, suitably chilled from being in my refrigerator. When I reached the imaging center I was injected
with a radioactive isotope, producing an immediate prickly
warmth throughout my body as I lay stretched horizontally,
ready to be received by the donut of the machine, open like a
great mouth.

That evening the doctor's nurse, with what I considered a lam-
entable lack of tact or compassion, called with preliminary results
and announced, quite casually, "It could be cancer or diverticulitis."

The latter I've been able to deal with quite successfully in the
past with antibiotics, but *cancer* has a different quality, even a
different color, in my mind. I was taken aback both by the raw
information and by the nonchalant way it was presented.

I've been wondering how doctors and nurses prepare themselves to announce test results to patients. Do they come straight
out with a dire prognosis, figuring that it's better to get it over
with, and if they turn out to be wrong and the patient has a
lesser ailment or none at all, that will be a nice surprise for
everyone? Or do they coat worrisome results with "maybe" or
"you need further evaluation before we'll know" so that the
news is broken "gently"? In the larger scheme of things it
doesn't make much difference, except to the patient's emotional
weather. But when a doctor has been your longtime health care

giver and you have become friends (she knows your body just as well or maybe better than you), it may be just as hard for her to make that announcement.

I'd been thinking almost glibly (and pretty theoretically) about the inevitability of aging and dying, but this unexpected news made it a lot more frontal, immediate, in my face, even though a more complete and definitive diagnosis had yet to be made.

Plans were made for further tests, and on the doctor's orders I canceled a trip to Texas with the Chrysostom Society (which eminent body last year elected me president) and notified the membership of the reason. A remarkable number of people immediately sprang into prayer for me.

Even more amazing, though at first I sensed a bit of disorientation in the face of the ominous possibilities, the next day I felt absolutely no anxiety. As an experiment, I tried to summon worry up like a genie out of a bottle, but nothing, not even a whiff of alarm, showed up in my emotional armamentarium. Might this possibly be because a lot of people are praying for me?

During my consult with Dr. Stiner, my gracious and skilled gastroenterologist, I got a lot more detailed information. He grades tumors by their size—"grapefruit, orange or golf ball." He said, "This is a very small golf ball." "Like a ping-pong ball?" I asked. "Exactly. Looks like it's near your ovary, so it could be ovarian cancer."

I'm not into astrology, but I'm remembering that the astrological sign for the Tropic of Cancer is a crab. With pincers. I prepare myself to be pincer-ed.

So I'm preparing for a sigmoidoscopy on Monday, the first step to ruling out colon cancer—the usual purge. Lord, purge my mind also of negative thoughts and fears.

I'm aware of more pain today. My imagination is working overtime to direct a kind of focused rebuke at the little crab nibbling at my innards. Alien and unwelcome, he's not about to stop without some strenuous method of ejection or sudden death.

So in my mind I'm oscillating between the image of the cheery ping-pong ball and the hostile little crab. Blood tests were taken today to detect any cancer markers. Waiting and not knowing is worse than even drastic action.

⁓

What do you do with a death sentence? We have all received it, whether acknowledged or not. Not just the possible news of a grave, impending illness, but the arrow that points "THIS WAY" every day of our lives since birth. All this past year I have been absorbing the fog-occluded view of some doorway through which I will leave my life and enter another territory.

Today I'm seeing the gynecologist, who with any luck may give me news about my future. Strange that I feel no apprehension. Just curiosity and intense interest.

Am I in denial? Yet this experience of suspicion and detective work is focusing my perceptions of life and is proving valuable in ways that I never expected.

*Later.* Nothing conclusive yet. An ultrasound is scheduled for next Monday. The gyne doctor is mildly encouraging—"With five normal pregnancies and births, and you being a nonsmoker all your life, I wouldn't worry too much!"

Yeah? OK for you to say. John and I want to shout, *Let's move on with this, whatever it is. Why the heck are we waiting around? Not knowing is almost more difficult than bad news.*

I'm reminded often of how impossible it is to be objective about one's own life. That ping-pong ball of a tumor—I'd like to pluck it out of my belly (lower left quadrant) and test it by bouncing it on the table and viewing it from inside and outside both: what it looks like, feels like, sounds like. A tiny explosion, or a hidden bomb. I want to smash it over the ping-pong net onto my opponent's side with a powerful serve that's impossible to return.

So I guess my responses are more visceral than I thought.

Facts are only limited aspects of reality to be included in any description. Day by day I've been portraying the steady plod through time as it happens. My daughter Marian, a skilled oncology nurse, in response to one of the updates I send my family, affirms by email what I've been feeling: "My patients talk about the time warp surrounding events like this. The need to know. The fear of knowing. The hurry-up urge frustrated by the wait for an open appointment. Such a push/pull time. Tough."

I read in a magazine today of death being viewed as "a gash in the fabric of the universe," which gives insufficient weight to the fact that death happens to each of us one at a time, thousands every moment. It may feel like a gash to me, the dying one, but it's only a tiny bubble in the foam of a breaker crashing on the shore.

See, I'm trying to be objective.

~

Wednesday, during lunch with the Yanceys, who were driving north to Whistler and stopped off in Bellingham for a visit, we filled them in on this unwieldy uncertainty. I told Philip how I'm writing it all down. "Yep, good material. Grist for the mill," he remarked.

He knows what he's talking about. He had his own recent brush with death when his neck was broken in a car accident. His books are alive with stories about the places he's been and the people he's met and the keen observations that resulted. That's how writers think: collecting experiences, pondering them, turning the lessons learned into words and stories.

Yes, as the plot of my life unfolds, it almost seems predetermined that this medical concern would make for fresh observations and provoke the questions behind the questions.

~

I got reintroduced to my interior by way of ultrasound this morning. This required drinking quantities of water that was not to be released until the procedure was over, resulting in some leakage anxiety on my part as I drove the twenty minutes to the imaging center. The tech who did the job was funny and friendly and searched my lower left quadrant diligently while I watched the shadowy movements, inscrutable to me, on the black-and-white screen. She got fairly frustrated, not at me but at not finding what she was looking for. She got hold of the radiologist, who joined the search on his adjoining screen.

Neither could find any trace of either of my ovaries (which they said would have shrunk with age to "the size of small raisins"). Nor of the "mass" that had mysteriously shown up last week on the CT scan. They told me, "You're a bit of a mystery." This is not, of course, the final word. Nor is it particularly encouraging.

But being a mystery, or in a state of mystery, is for me, I guess, where faith has to kick in. After all, faith is the ongoing work of the Christian soul. It is a continuing enterprise. Trust today isn't enough trust for tomorrow. It needs to be renewed daily as a conscious act on my part. This is a spiritual discipline.

I'm an Episcopalian because of mystery. The watertight systems of theological dogmatism held by some conservative circles is for me, to change the metaphor, like living in a fenced field while ignoring all the surrounding glorious landscape. In the mystery of restricted human living, longing toward God, I can grasp only an angel's wing feather, or a passing glint of God's glory in my peripheral vision. The vastness of future life in heaven has yet to be revealed.

I sometimes visualize the truths still hidden from me, what in the New Testament are designated "mysteries," as gathered like translucent beams of light high above me, in the groins and arches of this cathedral we call Christian faith. In one sense I myself am in that "cloud of unknowing." And in that knowledge gap I'm wondering if all the fervent prayers on my behalf have been already answered. Has the Healer been at work in my belly? And does he now continue to enlighten my soul?

And if all this has been a fuss about nothing, I need to ask what it has accomplished in me. What have I learned? Am I being newly fortified for the future?

In the last ten days I've had ample opportunity to reflect on the decor of four Bellingham clinic waiting rooms, where *waiting* is indeed the operative word. The term that seems to describe them all is *innocuous*. Pale, barely patterned wallpaper with tiny flecks of aqua or dusty rose or beige. Chairs comfortable enough to relax in and delude you into thinking you're an honored guest. Out-of-date tattered magazines that don't tell you anything you didn't already know. Bland artwork on the walls that defies art criticism. I gather all this is supposed to calm the impatient patient and reduce anxiety. It is, indeed, soporific.

I now have the opportunity to inspect a new clinic waiting room, that of a general surgeon. Since the other specialists have given up on me, I am to be delivered into hands that are able to penetrate (read *cut*) into my interior, rather than scanning from the skin in. Next Monday may or may not solve my mystery. But trust rather than apprehension continues to prevail!

It's more than helpful to have my personal consultant in Johnny, in Thailand, over Skype.

He understands my questions and can take more time to answer them than clinicians in an office. He is also extremely well informed, patient and understanding of his mom.

During these few days of waiting to see the surgeon on Monday, I'm fascinated rather than apprehensive.

It's way past Christmas, but the lines from Handel and his oratorio still sing in my head: "For as in Adam, all die" (minor chord, mournful tone and tempo), "even so in Christ shall all be made alive!" (excited, major chord, accelerated tempo). I've sung this multiple times in choirs, so the idea of a new kind of life, not just physical but total, is reviving again and again. I need to get it down out of my head into my bones. I need to claim fullness of life, in whatever form it presents itself from the hand of God.

And now something has powerfully presented itself from God's hand! This morning, before my appointment, my prayer group friends gathered round me as I sat on my office chair and wrapped me with love as they asked for God's wisdom for the doctor. It felt like a holy space.

And Dr. Fredette, the surgeon I saw today, a lovely man, pulled up the films of my interior onto his screen and meticu-lously pointed out to me the details of my gut. He felt that I should stop worrying about cancer. After all the rigorous searching and testing, the consensus is that they could find nothing but a possible diverticulitis attack, which I've had many times before and know how to deal with.

Though I have quite consciously been free from fear, I

sense relief. And for John it feels as if we've both been re-leased from prison after a life sentence. We went out for Thai food to celebrate.

Though being in a state of unknowing was a bit unnerving, I've learned a lot about trust and reality and issues of life and death. I feel as celebratory as if I'd had a birthday!

Of course, a birthday would mean that one more tide has risen and fallen on the beach of one's life. And one more year has been subtracted from one's life span.

*Birthday*

*So you change the water,*
*cut the stems at a clean angle,*
*add a bit of sugar, as if*
*mixing a drink for yourself*
*as well as the flowers.*

*You hope that moisture*
*will surge again up the green*
*stalks and flesh out*
*the lily petals' crumpled,*
*browning skin.*

*The mums last the longest.*
*Before that, you pluck*
*out the rosebuds, their pink*
*heads hanging in shame for*
*their failure to revive.*
*The ferns fronds are*
*resilient, but eventually*
*they shrivel. And you are left with*
*the container, "Made in England"*
*stamped on its ivory base.*[1]

Virginia Owens, in response to this poem I'd forwarded to her, sent me, by email, the image of a still life painting by the Dutch painter Ambrosius Bosschaert, an artfully arranged bouquet of flowers—lilies, peonies, tulips, narcissi—against a dark background. The key to the meaning of this picture is a small fly waiting on the ground beside the vase, and a caterpillar (presumably hungry) climbing up the tulip stem. Both speak of coming decay and bodily corruption.

≈

Several months later. I once again found myself awaiting test results. I'd had a follow-up CT scan, which, being interpreted, means that early in the day I had to drink two more large bottles of that barium contrast fluid that advertised its presence by gurgling and burbling its way south through my interior. And to protect my kidneys from clogging on the stuff, I ingested mystery pills at regular intervals before and after being slid into and out of the giant donut hole.

Then this morning I was greeted on the phone by Dr. Stiner's friendly nurse, Jane: "Good news, sweetie. Everything looks fine from your test. Whatever it was is gone. Nothing to worry about. Have a great day!"

"Oh, yes! I will. And you too!"

So. After all those tests and other indignities I can feel "normal" again. Thank God. Truly.

≈

But sometimes the subliminal pressure and anxiety of a cancer diagnosis reasserts itself. It feels like a healed scar on my soul. Thinking along those lines, sometimes I pause and review my scars, which are a bit like a history of my long life. There's the scar from the emergency appendectomy I had at the age of eleven, in Toronto. It was touch and go, before antibiotics, and my appendix had actually burst, but they managed to remove the offending organ before sepsis set in.

You can't actually see the site of the tonsillectomy I had at the age of twenty. In those days tonsils were suspected to be the cause of many evil physical conditions. I remember the post-surgery thrill of being offered ice cream to soothe the throat-pain aftermath.

In my late forties I had a hysterectomy. They did it the old way, with a vertical incision. The resulting scar tissue actually helps hold my belly in place! After all, I'd had five children and really didn't need that old uterus any more. No more birth control necessary. No more monthly periods. Hallelujah!

Later, in my fifties, I had a knuckle on my right foot debrided, the big toe joint shaved, after it became swollen enough with arthritis to force a change of shoe style. I learned that *debrided* comes from a French word basically meaning "unbridled." That runaway horse of arthritis has been kicking me much of my life!

Both my knees have thin white scar lines running from my lower thighs down across my kneecaps to my shins, evidence of where a skilled orthopedic surgeon opened me up, removed my old knee joints and put in constructions of titanium and ceramic that allow me to walk strongly and without too much pain. Ditto for the scar on my left ankle: it was replaced several years later and stabilized with steel pins.

I have scars on my right hand where our black cat Gigabite got irritated and dug into me while I was taking him to the vet for shots. And on my left forefinger tip, nearly sliced off while peeling an avocado. I had to hold the finger up in the air for hours to stem the bleeding.

A more recent scar comes from the moment last year after a friend of my brother's rode over and suggested I mount his motorbike for a photo—to make a visual record of my intrepidity. What he forgot to mention to me was that the exhaust pipe was still burning hot. It singed the inside of my right calf right through my jeans and on further inspection revealed a blister the size of a small balloon that took nearly a year to heal. It's just a whitish patch now, but reminds me what a showoff I was.

Last summer I underwent a bowel resection in which the part of my colon still infested with diverticuli was removed and the severed ends sewn together. Though this surgery was done arthroscopically, with three tiny incisions, my belly button was discarded in the process. I sent the following poem to Dr. Fredette, with my compliments:

*It was the surgeon's duty*
*to do the drastic deed*
*that cut away my beauty,*
*the helpless little bead*
*of skin that once embellished*
*the region at my waist.*
*Oh, it was dearly cherished,*
*and now it's gone to waste.*
*I miss it, and I'm grieving*
*for that which has been cut,*
*well-knowing that its leaving*
*will benefit my gut.*

I've noticed after buying fruit at the supermarket, apples, grapefruit, pears, glorious in their displays of color and texture, that the scarred fruits are inevitably sweeter than those with perfect skins.

Wounds heal into scars, tissue that is tough enough to hold tight for as long as needed. Hidden wounds of the spirit don't always heal as completely as flesh. But when they do, I often think again of St. Paul's words to the Corinthians, "God of all healing counsel! He comes alongside us when we go through hard times, and before you know it, he brings us alongside someone else who is going through hard times so that we can be there for that person just as God was there for us" (2 Corinthians 1:3 *The Message*).

My own pains and difficulties and the resultant healing have been instructive; they come in handy when I meet someone with the same problems and can genuinely sympathize (a word that links *same* and *pathos*). And prayer for whatever needs healing in me becomes a springboard for me to pray for individuals worldwide who need the same curative touch from God.

# 15

## Course Corrections

*How to harness a critical spirit?* Today, again, I had deeply uncharitable thoughts about someone who frequently annoys me, and though I bit my lip and refrained from exploding or pointing this out aloud, I'm reminded of Jesus' words about the thoughts of our hearts being as potent as our outward actions. They're like a bitter drug that eats at us like heartburn.

When I speak of being *critical* I'm not using the word in its best sense—discerning between good and bad literature or music or art, or between right and wrong action—but about my meanness of spirit when I focus on someone else's failings and bad behavior, or lack of love, and I almost enjoy it. I sense that this reflects my own lack of charity.

But then I wonder, is that response a kind of negative mind control, a denial of aggravation in which I train myself to see everything in its most positive light and attribute to the irritant the sweetest of motives? How honest is that? Is it a truly godly way for me to maintain a pure heart?

Might not the reminder of my own judgmental thoughts directed at another human being become a continuing avenue for prayer, for penitence and correction? If I never harbored a negative impulse or thought or recognized their reality—an unearthly state to be sure—would I almost be placing myself outside of the mercy of God?

So, I'm realizing again, there's a big difference between a New Year's resolution and a Lenten discipline. The first tends to be in one's own best interest. The other is for God's satisfaction.

❧

Today Arabella is here, in all her three-year-old great-granddaughterly charm. She is settled on my couch, tucked under a fleece blanket and surrounded by her "children," the stuffed toys that accompanied her to our house. She is watching *The Lion King* with focused scrutiny on the screen that doesn't prevent her from asking "Why?" from time to time.

*Why?* is the cry of young children getting acquainted with the enigmas of the world. It is also the cry of the elderly. Why is my life moving to an end? Why did God put me here in the first place? And have I fulfilled his purpose for my life?

With regard to Lenten discipline, I need to focus very continually and intentionally on patience. I'm finding that remembering God's patience with me and my foibles assists my focus on patience with others. I expect things to be done logically and efficiently, and when they aren't, my self-denial has to come to the fore and remember that the fact that things aren't done my way doesn't necessarily mean they're done badly or wrongly or with flawed intention.

❧

In the Scripture readings from our Sunday lectionary, I am so struck by the continuing narrative of thirst, and water to satisfy that thirst: the parched Hebrew people in the desert complaining to Moses about their lack, and Psalm 95, which reflects on that very incident. In Romans 5, the purpose for suffering is to turn

us to God, whatever our need, and we remember the story of the
Samaritan woman at the well from whom Jesus begs a drink, and
then tells her about the "spring of water gushing up to everlasting life" (John 4:14). Jesus widened his invitation, telling this
woman that anyone who would drink from this inner spring
would never thirst again.

Yet I do thirst. Perhaps my longing for God's water will be
satisfied only when I can drink of the river in heaven that flows
from God's throne, in that everlasting life.

And then our choir anthem, "Like as a hart desireth the water
brooks, so longeth my soul for thee." (We did wonder if the
youth in our congregation would know what a "hart" was.)

❧

Yesterday afternoon, forgoing our usual Sunday afternoon
naps, John and I went to a concert with the legendary pianist
Garrick Ohlsson and the Whatcom Symphony. A great thick
bear of a man, 6'4" tall, Ohlsson played the Brahms Piano Con-
certo no. 1 in C minor with such delicacy and precision, coupled
with such strength and sureness, it seemed miraculous. Knowing
the piece well in our heads, we were both utterly carried out of
ourselves by his interpretation. That too filled a thirst in us, for
beauty, for artistry. He made it new as well water.

❧

Today, an email message from an organization known as
Training Summits, inviting me to become part of a team of ex-
ecutives and visionaries—trainers whose agenda it is to help
their trainees to "outperform."

I'm willing to admit that there's a certain value in efficient, forward-looking planning and training, but the word *outperform* bothers me somehow. *Schadenfreude* is all too likely to happen when one aims for the top; the news of someone else's failure to achieve boosts our own sense of "outperformance."

It may be true that the whole human effort to get ahead may often be because the only choice these days is between survival and impoverishment. But I suspect it's what I deal with still in my own efforts—the urge to outperform and thus become exceptional, which far too easily slides into arrogance and hubris.

I responded to the invitation thus: that I hope to grow innerly rather than outperformingly. And I unsubscribed from the organizational blog.

❧

John and I were invited to participate in a lunchtime "conversation" with theologian/philosopher Alvin Plantinga hosted by the philosophy department at Western Washington University. In the Q&A session I was brash enough to ask a couple of questions to which Dr. Plantinga gave reasonable and respectful answers. We were surrounded by a multitude of male philosophers and academics whose questions were so much more intellectual and sophisticated than mine, I was prepared to be embarrassed.

Why do I test the sound of my own voice like this, even when that voice sometimes comes out as a bit husky due to postnasal drip? I think it's because sometimes I'm helped to understand internally what my question really is, just by trying to articulate it.

In this case I asked this mighty man of philosophy whether, in his opinion, the beauty of the creation is an aspect of divine grace. He said, of course it is, but there's lots more that's beautiful beside ferns and flowers. Mathematics, for instance.

I'd often heard of the so-called elegance of pure mathematics, but I am too mathematically challenged to have fully appreciated this.

I suppose what I contribute vocally in public may sometimes have value. In choir I'll complain, "That measure is too high for the altos." Or "Could we hear how that melody goes again?" But I've been noticing how often I respond to or baldly correct someone else's statement of fact or opinion, "Well, no . . ." Or, "Actually, what he said was . . ." Or, "No, no, no, that's not true." Or, "How can you say that? Weren't you listening?"

I need tempering, like glass. I need to accept more, amend more gently, listen rather than assert. Especially when it is God who speaks.

 

I spent an hour plucking weeds this morning. With any gradual warmth comes the springing up of not only the plants we invite and cultivate but also the wild, rapacious ones that we try to eliminate, that raise our ire and increase our backache from too much bending.

The trouble with weeding is that it's never finished. Pull up a weed and what you have left is a kind of negative space that was once occupied but is now blank. No one but you can tell that your work has accomplished anything.

But is the weed-free space really negative? I think of a painting with a wide frame or matte board surrounding it, showing it up, directing our focus to the image, not the empty space. Or a poem on a page, the words in black type on white paper that is saying "Don't look at me, read the poem I'm surrounding."

A bit like sins, or character flaws—when they've been eliminated and the individual's penchant for error corrected, who's to know what struggle was involved, what surrender of will to God, what internal compass has been reset? But the virtue, the shining, of a disciplined, gifted life is there to be witnessed without the distraction of human foibles and failings.

～

But OK, let me be a contrarian. In a garden like ours, a careful landscape arrangement of native plants and pleasingly placed rocks and shrubs and perennials, and a kiwi vine–covered trellis sheltering ferns, hostas, iris, lilies of the valley, bunchberries, there are enough open spaces to invite the intrusion of those hardy specimens we call weeds, denizens of the wild. (We grew this garden patch from scratch, which allowed us to plan what we wanted rather than reconstructing what someone else had left abandoned.)

Over the fifteen years of our human supervision this project has flourished. People driving by stop and comment. Pedestrians enjoy our little landscape, as do we. Until the arrival of a robust pea vine. Wild grass. Bindweed. Oxalis. Horsetails and thorny blackberries (they are the worst; it seems almost impossible to keep them down). And other unknown, unidentified interlopers. I grind my teeth and get to work to make them realize they are *personae non grata*.

Yet in spite of myself I've always had a certain respect for weeds. Their ability to survive and flourish in spite of all efforts to banish them. Their perky hopefulness that suggests that despite all adversaries they will survive. I admire their ability to proliferate. And I'm in awe of the profuse and often beautiful blooms they produce—buttercups, day lilies, wild geraniums, dandelions, wild violets, hollyhocks, fireweed—and the nourishing fodder they provide for beasts of the field.

Some weeds are humble, creeping low along the soil. (And they flourish even in poor, dry, dusty soil.) Others are showy and brazen. They always have green stems and leaves—the color of growth, my favorite color. And, they are created by God—integral parts of his wilderness garden.

I think, too, of people I might characterize as "weeds" in my life. They may differ from me politically, or theologically, or philosophically, or morally. They may gossip, or offend me by their crude speech or manners, or fail to live up to their commitments. Yet each of them has a place to fill on this planet. Each is a product of divine creation. Each is loved by God.

Sometimes I ponder: Am I a weed or a more domesticated herb? No matter, God's rain and sun blesses the just and the unjust, equally.

# 16

# Companions on the Way

*I've received a new message,* a reflection on time (that integral, inescapable factor in aging), sent from Fr. Malcolm Guite, my singer/poet/priest friend in England. This is his voiced reflection on the life of a pioneer missionary to China in the sixteenth century.

> *This candle wears away before whose light*
> *I practice my calligraphy,*
> *This candle might be counting down the time*
> *That flickers between passing lights and darks.*
> *Time in the east is not marked off in ticks.*
> *It is not measured by our western clocks.*
> *Time is a stream that falls and fills*
> *And wears like water on the rocks.*

As I drive north to Tsawwassen, just sixty miles across the Canadian border, to see my spiritual director, the clear, sunny sky, and the way the bare trees' and bushes' branches and twigs stood out in exceptionally clear-cut detail against the clarity, seemed as if seen through a lens. Two eagles sat beside each other, high in a roadside tree.

A kind of exhilaration set in. I felt lifted, as if the entire planet, its rounded, throbbing globe, were beneath me, supporting me, and the vast blue space above me invited me to breathe and feel free and vibrantly alive in a kind of infinity. Even in my car the sense of oneness with creation was palpable.

Remembering, pondering this later, I was reminded of the comment of Ruth Pitter, C. S. Lewis's poet friend, about such dumbfounding moments: "What is this thing? . . . Could it be, after all, a hint of something more real than this life—a message from reality—perhaps a particle of reality itself? If so, no wonder we hunt it so unceasingly and never stop desiring and pining for it."[1]

Very occasionally I have had these moments, these "showings." I can number them on one hand, when heaven and earth have been joined, pulsing with a kind of translucence, and I am an ecstatic part of it all.

This kind of experience usually happens in solitude, out in the open and away from normal life. It's impossible to plan, coming from quite literally God knows where. I've tried to duplicate it, returning to the same place in the same kind of weather at the same time of year as when it has taken hold of me before. But all I can regain is the memory of a memory.

I wonder if St. Paul, "caught away" after his conversion, unable to describe it, had this kind of God-given vision. Words are utterly inadequate to express it.

I've begun the second half of the fisherman knit sweater I'm making for Wade (who once admitted, "No one's ever knitted a sweater for me"). The jade-green wool I found in our local knit shop pleases me immensely. But the complexities of the pattern, especially as it is just being established again as I start on the front (I've completed the back and one sleeve, and it has lain fallow for a while), take a great deal of concentration, with many repeats within repeats as all the different patterns and stitches are formed, row by row.

It's a bit like Celtic knotwork, with no visible beginning and ending of lines, which coil and weave over and under, in and out of each other. I remember noticing an ancient ivy growth covering a stone wall in Wales and wondering if the intersecting vines, or the spreading, interlacing roots of an ancient oak, gave rise to the early Celtic sense of intricate design patterns.

I find it quite thrilling to finally figure out how the knitting pattern works, having the right number of stitches and beginning to see my effort grow into something real and ingenious. Now I can move forward with confidence that this will be a successful project!

Knitting is a lifelong domestic activity that continues to keep me grounded in physical reality. I can knit as I watch TV. Or sit with friends. Or on the plane as I traveled to my granddaughter Shelly's wedding one winter weekend. (They allow knitting needles on planes once again.) The great joy of wool growing into a garment that will comfort and ornament someone's body (and perhaps remind them of me)! It brings me the gratification one gets from doing so many "simple" things that don't at first feel so simple. Making bread. Growing tomatoes. Writing poems. Taking photographs of the moss on a rock this morning. Tent-camping. Meditating.

Working incrementally. I'm on the last stretch, the final lap, approaching the longed-for frontier, fulfilling the mandate of the ultimate professional knitter's goal of finishing a sweater. The front is done. The back is done, and one sleeve lies on a chair waiting for its partner. It goes a row at a time, with a decrease at each end of every other row of the raglan shoulder of the sleeve, so the number of stitches on each row is fewer as I move north on the arm. It sounds tedious. It feels slow, but somehow it's triumphant. The excitement increases!

What is the difference between pride and satisfaction? Am I feeling superior to nonknitters? John looks at the work with wonder—"How on earth do you know how to do that?" I tell him it's only by being obedient to the instructions. (And being willing to rip it out and start over if I make a mistake.)

≈

This is, I know, an old issue for me—the need to feel needed, appreciated, wanted. This hunger is temporarily satisfied when a journal accepts a poem or essay, or a composer asks for permission to set a poem of mine to music. (Right now I have British, Canadian and US musicians at work on musical settings. Some of the results are delightful. Some are a bit avant-garde and seem dissonant to me. I know that's a matter of taste, and my tastes aren't universal!)

I know such gratification won't last long, though I have a hunch that the music will last longer than books or journals or other print media as technology takes over the publishing industry with ebooks and other formats. Music will continue to sing within us as long as we have something to sing about. And in our ears, as long as we have ears to listen with.

≈

Yesterday, a picturesque drive back from Whidbey Island with its alternating pasturelands and sudden lakes and hills. And Deception Pass, where the tide boils through the narrow entry from sea into Puget Sound and back again. I always park and walk and gasp from the high bridge that spans the gap.

I was traveling down to Ft. Casey, where the current cohort of student writers is gathered for the residency to work on their MFAs. Fr. Dave Denny leads morning worship and sometimes invites me to participate, this time reflecting on the appropriate topic "Age."

So many of my favorite friends are there in one place as faculty for the program—Jeanne, Jeanine, Gina, Leslie, Paula, Robert, Greg—and after the evening's entertainment (a wildly funny student contest of comedic poems), we women departed and settled for the evening in the living room of one of the little old houses erected long ago to house the bachelor officers who staffed the fort.

A prolonged, thoughtful and wide-ranging conversation ensued, about our lives, our writing and more. We all long for these connections, spread as we are around the country. We tend to meet at varied venues and conferences for writers.

I was housed for the night in Unit 8 in an upstairs bedroom. Though tastefully restored and decorated, these buildings are old enough to have glass windows that blur and distort the scenery beyond them. Through the glass the old-fashioned streetlamp outside seemed to have developed a kink in its metal lamppost. The grass and bushes were a swirl of new green. There were surreal clouds in the sky.

I realize that what I want, what I need, is an unambiguous view. I need to see what *is* in the world, without a protective or warped lens, with no funhouse mirror. I want the lens of my eye to be crystal clear, but also, as I get older, I want my inner perceptions to be true to visible and invisible realities, whether or not my physical eyes are dim or cloudy. I like St. Paul's prayer: that "the eyes of your heart" be "enlightened" (Ephesians 1:18).

Warning notice on the back of the second-story bedroom door of this little house: "In case of fire, exit through the bedroom window onto the roof." And then what? The leap of faith?

&

Two "sightings" within a day of each other. One, the film *Of Gods and Men* viewed by John and me at our local independent film center. The other the death of Osama bin Laden, flashed across the world like a lightning bolt. I can't help contrasting them.

In the film, which is about a group of Trappist monks in a small monastery in an Algerian hamlet, the monks are threatened by Islamic extremists and eventually captured and beheaded, though the flame of their faith is never extinguished. The film occupies itself with the process of discernment, in the group and individually, about whether to stay put with the local townspeople—people amongst whom they minister in spite of the danger—or return to France for safety in the home base of their order.

Brother Luc, the elderly, grumpy but tender-hearted physician-monk, among the others, decides to stay. He tells them, "I'm not afraid of capture. I'm not afraid of torture. I'm not afraid of death. No matter what happens, I'm a free man."

I can't help but contrast that with Osama bin Laden's choice to be penned up for seven years for presumed safety in his Pakistani stronghold, confined to a compound with walls so high that he could not be seen, confined to a small room, his whole view of the world seen through the lens of an ancient TV. Huddled up in a blanket against the cold. And in the end taken out by US Navy Seals against his will. He'd given up his freedom for safety, but his safety wasn't safe enough.

Safety versus freedom. We each have to decide. It's another paradox, but perhaps in Christ we can ultimately have both?

~

Here's a contrast. Yesterday, driving through town, I saw a group of people being escorted along the sidewalk. Most of them clearly had "special needs." Some had cerebral palsy. Others looked like teenagers with Down syndrome. A few were almost being carried by caregivers, possibly because they were too weak to be ambulatory on their own.

I've seen these clusters of folks before, on the same street. I suppose experiencing the fresh air, being part of the human activities along the streets and shops, moving around, feeling a part of some forward movement, contributes to their physical and emotional health.

And yet these excursions seem so limited, so brief in terms of life spans. What do they mean more than momentary relief? Do they do more than simply add to a series of similar moments that may gleam briefly in a safe but limited life?

And ultimately, to what end are these short-lived experiences? In other words, what is the significance of the present moment when the rest of life looks so drastically limited?

~

This afternoon, a sweet sigh of relief. I'd been kind of nervous about leading a poetry class at the Wade King Elementary School today, much more anxious than I would have been teaching college students. Tiffany, their teacher, reassured me that these fourth-graders had been learning about poetry and other essentials like imagination and creativity and were duly excited about meeting "a real live poet." (I guess there aren't that many around? Or maybe they're not that visible within that particular culture?)

I'd cut short the green stem of the still glorious flowerhead of Queen Anne's lace from my Mother's Day bouquet from Robin and placed it in water in a bud vase as an object to be attended to. I hoped it would stimulate some engaging young poets and their fresh, unfiltered words.

And we had a marvelous time together! The kids all clustered around on the floor, or at their desks, eager, intelligent, responsive, funny. I found myself relating to them easily in spite of all the years since my own kids and grandkids had been that age. They ask the typical questions: When did you start writing poems? (Around six.) And its follow-up: How long ago was that? (Seventy-eight years. I anticipated incredulity, but apparently the idea of being eighty-four is too abstract to have meaning for human beings this young.)

We conversed about colors and shapes and memories and imagination and how our senses inform our minds. They wrote poems about the flower in the vase and read them back to us all—with no self-conscious shyness at all.

Time came for their next class, and reluctantly we had to say goodbye, but they want me to come back and keep going. I am pleased that this particular anxiety has been put to rest. Also happy that I can still connect with the very young, and maybe give them a new understanding that imagination doesn't end with age.

# 17

# The Grass Under Our Feet

*A winter garden is* a pretty sad place, drab and brown with rotting leaves and twigs, destitute of green and growth but for the moss that somehow thrives even after being frozen. It velvets over the harshness of the granite boulders around which our native plants are artfully arranged.

Today Liz, our "gardening angel" who has been overseeing the garden's health and welfare for several months, came to groom and trim. The sun actually shone at a low angle, and the sky brightened after the days of heavy rain that had turned our creek into a wild, foaming cascade below the garden. Liz cut back the dark, dead upright stems of the ornamental grasses, the crocosmia, astrancia and peonies, and pruned the potentilla.

At this time of year it's sometimes possible to see tiny green buds on certain bushes. It's the increased light that prompts the green to grow. Light equals life.

*The deer, the deer, the rampant deer,*
*We see them there, we see them here,*
*And soon we'll see them everywhere.*

Soon the young deer will be born in the forest. They are experimenters, these charming spotted fawns uneducated in matters of haute cuisine in deer society, who will try anything, nibbling even at salal and bitter rhododendrons, until they learn better. I once wrote a poem about Bellingham wildlife, singling out the deer, slugs and food moths that have raised my ire.

Last year John strung wires between the horizontal bars of the fence that divides the garden from the ravine. We thought it might discourage the deer, those beautifully innocent creatures that climb up to our property along the creek bed. But of course they simply practice leaping nimbly over the fence into the forbidden preserve. They are protected by the county, which provides no protection for the humans and their agricultural efforts at taming the wild.

≈

St. Patrick's Day. I am not Irish, nor am I remotely related to George Bernard Shaw, yet without thinking I put on a green sweater and green earrings this morning. And when I drove downtown, all the traffic lights were green! The whole world seems to be greening, the days getting longer and lighter, the rain continuing to nourish the earth. I am feeling fresh, and refreshed. I long for the whole world to grown even greener, including me!

*Everywhere*
*buds are budding,*
*bees are being.*
*All around me,*
*floods are flooding,*
*& I'm eyeing*
*what I'm seeing*

*in the light*
*where light is*
*lighting, I'm*
*delighting.*

It's the first day of spring, the vernal equinox, when day and night face off against each other—if you view them as adversarial—or through a more positive lens, when light and darkness are equally paired and partnered in our annual cycle. Listened on NPR to Debussy's "Printemps" (Spring), evocative music that starts with mournful slowness and rises at the finale to a kind of green abandon.

Other rumors of spring are murmuring across the face of the earth. Even in our cooler microclimate, at the top of the Coronado hill, here and there one can glimpse the purple beak of a crocus, a blue anemone, an aconite opening its yellow face to the sun, geese flying north (we're on an avian flyway), an eagle circling, cherry blossoms popping up their miniature heads, like pink goosebumps, out of bare branches on the Alabama Street cherry trees. Along all the highways, snuff-colored twigs are swelling up from below, from the rain-soaked ground, root to trunk to branch to bud, bursting with spring juices that flesh out the trees with the promise of leaves. (Don't ask me how I know the color of snuff; I just do; I believe it's kind of tobacco-colored.)

Then today I spotted a mustard-yellow Corvette with neon-green hubcaps dodging in and out of traffic like a large and agile insect. I briefly lusted after it until I remembered that this is Lent, and such lust is inappropriate. Not only is Lent a season of self-examination to prepare oneself for Jesus' death and resurrection, but the word *lent* means "slow" in French. Just like the gradual lengthening of light.

Nothing stirs me to write new poetry more than reading the poems of others, letting their rhythms and images perplex, confound, enlighten and enliven me, stirring new resonances, like vibrations of some stringed instrument that I myself am being played.

Yesterday, for instance, the new issue of *Poetry* arrived, full of experiment and commentary, poets familiar or fresh all speaking the complex language of literature, and today I started four new poems, experiments on my computer screen that keep calling for additions and revisions. It remains to be seen whether any of them has life beyond itself, but getting words onto a notebook or a screen makes me feel like a spider beginning to weave a new web, drawing silk out of her own abdomen.

Speaking of words, Carolyn Forché comments in this new issue of *Poetry* that she finds in the term *experience* a reference to the Latin *experiri*, a kind of forward movement with a hint of peril, like crossing a suspension bridge, or a border—a test that one must undergo, a trial that does not leave one untouched, unchanged.[1]

≈

"Now the green blade riseth, / Wheat that springeth green." Our congregation sang this wonderful French spring carol in today's Sunday morning worship. And along all the roadsides as we drive, we are glorying in the grasses and all the early, glowing green that is filling up the spaces between branches and earth and sky. This is a time of year when the whole world glistens, fresh, hung with diamonds after the showers, emitting its own variety of subdued radiance. And then the sun opens up like an eye and it all comes vividly alive, shouting its joy.

As often, but especially this year, the rain has seemed endless, unremitting. But I know this: it is the wetness, the moistened, humus-rich soil, that makes for greenness. Each grass blade that pierces up into the light is thirsty. Each vine along our garden trellis lengthens by inches because it drinks from the root below.

I love the conclusion of the song: "Love is come again with wheat that springeth green." It is God's grace, his love for us and his creation, that brings this revival of green life to our senses, our souls.

Even in the dimness of our garage where, until it's safe to plant outside, we store our tomato planter bin all winter with last year's soil, I notice an anonymous green shoot (not a tomato) poking up. It has a minimum of dampness to grow from, but there it is in that gray sterile environment. I also have an old photo of a tulip blooming out of a slit in the side of a compost bin. New life and growth will not be foiled.

Last year was when we started four new clematis vines in square wooden planters on our deck, encouraged by compost from our bin. The plants did pretty well, and we enjoyed some fabulous purple, white and pink blooms in the late summer and fall. This spring, in trimming back some of last year's dead stems, I discovered, days later, that I'd severed the main stalk on one plant, and all the new green buds above it were drooping and dying.

Heartsick (I get emotionally attached to my plants; they feel like my children), I cut the whole thing back to the ground, hoping for new growth. Lo and behold, today I noticed a bright, happy young shoot poking up from the soil. It's hard to suppress that kind of buoyant life. In herbs. In humans.

*Later.* Still in my nightgown, I creep onto the deck to check on the clematis planters. The new sprout of stalk from the stub of the one I cut down is now more than a foot high, busting out with leaves and new growth. The leaves are so fresh they are

almost transparent, oval green windows for the morning sun to
shine through. Like the importunate widow, this plant will not
be discouraged. I'm no widow, but oh, my Lord, I'm importunate for more light, more life, more leaves, more increase in
wisdom, more grace.

After two more days, I notice the upstart clematis has risen to
the level of the first rung of its frame and has tenderly wound a
stemmed leaf around it, as if hooking an arm around the shoulder
of a friend. I know I tend to anthropomorphize my plants. I feel
such identification with them, such fellow feeling. Maybe I was
originally intended to be an herb! Clearly this didn't happen. At
least I want to tend the Garden.

In an erudite and absorbing *New Yorker* article called "Other
Worlds" (largely about scientific explorations into the possible
existence of multiple universes), I came across the statement,
"Physics has surprised us with the [fact] that . . . the universe,
if viewed from the outside, is beige."[2]

I scribbled in my journal:

*So, we're all an inoffensive neutral
and our colors mere mirages—
effects of the way light charges through
the prisms of us and our objects which
are made of subatomic particles
anyway.*

*Nothing significant here.
Is this a God's eye view?
I'd have hoped
we were a bit more vivid—
more substantial substrates for
our sentient minds and bodies.*

But then, with that note of disillusionment heavily in mind, John and I drove down on Saturday to Mt. Vernon in the Skagit Valley, where hundreds of acres of tulips were opening up in turn and blooming brilliantly. Massed red, yellow, purple, pink, flame-color, parrot tulips, miniatures in flowerbeds intersected by fruit trees, also in bloom. Even on an ancient apple tree, scaled with moss and lichen, scarlet tulips were growing like clots of color in the crooks among the branches.

Such dazzling color is too real to be washed out, hosed away like blood from a murder scene, by the theories of physicists. Even in the rain, with the grayed-out Cascade Range in the far background, the fields of such vivid intensity keep filling my mind and memory with their own pigment. All of us continue to be painted on by the brush of God. This kind of unexpected beauty is salvific.

With the relief of having nothing scheduled until choir practice tonight, I lie in bed, watching a pale blue cloudless sky through the skylight above our bed, window open for the cool silky air, my body just the right temperature under the duvet to relax and rest, though awake.

The contrast of chill and warmth make for perfection; each seems to enhance the magic of the other. Though there are no clouds above me, foggy wisps of words float through my mind unhindered and sometimes grow into something coherent enough to kick-start a poem, when I get the energy to throw aside the covers, make notes in my bedside journal and glide downstairs to my computer to start this vivid new thing.

Today's forecast is for a high (gasp!) in the 60s.

*Flowerhead*

*Grandmama crocheted doilies*
*for breakfast trays, embroidered*
*tablecloths, stitched antimacassars*
*for the back of his upholstered chair*
*to protect the fabric from*
*my granddad's ancient, oily head.*

*It's July, eighty-five years later. Like galaxies,*
*like the blaze of fireworks on the Fourth,*
*the tablecloth of Queen Anne's lace*
*embroiders the meadow.*

*No matter how lovely, age happens.*
*This flowered lace will bend its thin bones*
*from exploding stars to wired cages*
*for small insects, the browned flowerets*
*bowing to the center,*
*honoring each other's spent life.*[3]

The incremental life continues. Ticking by in minutes, hours, days. I wonder why it seems important to me to notice how the number of vitamin pills in a bottle is diminished, one by one, every morning. Or realize that my hair is an inch longer than two weeks ago. Or that my legs need shaving. Again. The forward movement of living is unstoppable, unretraceable. Better make sure your decisions and actions are for the best.

It's a constant part of my life to check growing plants for signs of buds and growth, to long for the final opening of a flower. What excitement I feel as the days grow longer, a few minutes per day, as the laying of a new gas line along Lakeway Drive is progressing—being outlined and excavated and pipe laid in the trench like a long green snake, which is now being filled in and paved, and moving on up the hill with about ten large and complicated machines at work, all orange metal and rust and gears and windowed cabs high above the apparatus!

Every day as I pass this production line, with the road workers brandishing their signs that say "slow" or "stop," I am feeling satisfaction at the work that has been finished up to *here*. And tomorrow it may be up to *here*. How well it seems to be going!

Then I ask myself, *Do I need reconstruction? Am I willing to exert myself on this upward ascent? What keeps me from giving up?* But I know that patience and persistence are virtues I value for all kinds of expeditions, including climbing.

~

John and I are already getting restless. We hope we're ready for this major upheaval to a new home.

These are all signs, all evidences of transition, of change. I feel such strong identification with all such processes of growth. Perhaps constructive movement forward signifies hope. Perhaps it is myself I am really hoping for, to make sure I am not static or fossilized. That I don't end up like an abandoned, ragged blackberry patch. That even at this stage of my life progress can be fluid and life-giving and fertile and provide a means of protection and comfort to others.

### Credo

*I believe in Free Enterprise, Pride of Place*
*Fiscal Responsibility, The Middle Ages,*
*Seasonal Allergies, Queen Anne's Lace,*
*Undying Love, The Communion of Saints,*

*The Golden Ratio, Due Process, Outer Space,*
*The Diet of Worms, The Bay of Fundy,*
*The Statue of Liberty, The Human Race,*
*The Freedom of the Press, The Milky Way,*
*The Four Seasons, The Commonplace,*
*Pinot Grigio, The Bermuda Triangle,*
*The Golden Years, Prevenient Grace.*[4]

Months later, the house is complete. The gutters are attached, and the lights work. The deck railings have been installed. The building inspector has come and gone and proclaimed all systems go. It's time for the penultimate stripping down (I say penultimate because the ultimate still looms ahead), in the way climbers in thin air must abandon everything weighty that would slow them down or cause extra fatigue.

We take a planning morning with Mark and Robin, Johnny and Christa, John and me, to develop a moving schedule. We're not hiring a mover—it's only three and a half miles from the "old" house to the new one, so the strong volunteer arms and hands of friends and family will hoist the beds, couches, tables into a rental truck. It almost feels like a mountain rescue, with stretchers and medics in attendance!

We hope the rain keeps off on Tuesday, moving day.

Our old house is full of things "saved" for the future. Art objects, curios, family silver, furniture, bone china. We hope to share some of these oddments with our descendants, hoping they'll understand the history invested in them. We empty file cabinets of old papers and records. We shred some of our more ancient tax documents. We realize how little of this we really need.

When Johnny and Christa committed themselves to living in Thailand and working toward humanitarian aid, they were nudged into rethinking the difference between wants and needs. They were moving to a foreign culture with vastly different living requirements. I quote from the blog Johnny wrote about their transition:

> In the run-up to moving back to Thailand, one notable experience is the shift from acquiring to dispersing. I'm no shopper, but the sight of that lonely single suitcase I am bringing has firmly silenced the voice within that whispers so constantly about what I should buy next. My inner Hoover has been unplugged. In ensuing silence Christa and I are left to consider what I will call "the packer's dilemma." Namely, if we wear all our clothes at once when boarding the airplane in order to fit our best books in our suitcase, will we be able to bend enough to fit into our Economy seats? Can you layer shoes?
>
> In these last months we have been forced to consider the question that advertisers really hoped we wouldn't: "What really matters?" All movers face this, but ironically our suitcase constraint brought on by routing our flight through Europe, and a decision not to ship things overseas, brings freedom. Because what we really bring to Thailand and Burma for the next few years is . . . ourselves. No amount of baggage can replace what we carry within. Although we need a few tools, mostly what we need is the willingness to go, to see and listen, to work alongside others, to act when possible with clarity of purpose, to persist and to unite our imperfect selves with the ones we find working to meet an astounding need. . . . I'm convinced that it isn't our money that will accomplish the work we go to do, nor—beyond a few needed

things—our household items. We hope to consolidate our prosperous lives, sitting stiffly in that plane, into what character and skills we hold within and our two suitcases of chosen stuff. And of course, Divine Providence . . .

So there. That's what John and I need to consider—what to do with our collections of stuff? We too count on divine providence, but what is my husband to do with his carved elephants (everyone gives him elephants; he once headed an expedition over the Alps with an elephant!)? What am I to do with the antique desk I found in the 1960s in a Chicago collectibles store that I stripped of five coats of thick black paint down to its satiny carved wood? And the old-fashioned side chair I paired it with and painstakingly caned? They fit uneasily in a modern setting, but they're like a pair of comfortably worn hiking shoes—I'm not ready to abandon them. The paintings and photographs that have caught my eye with their shape and color and had framed, including several from Lauren, my gifted artist granddaughter: there are so many, and not enough new empty walls to hang them on.

I sort the books in my study bookshelves, many signed by their authors. The boxes of volumes saved to be reread: will there be time to enjoy them, gain from them all? We ditch the old music cassettes, the obsolete USB cables, the tattered instruction manuals for our outworn appliances. Stuff is everywhere in piles to be boxed or shipped or set out for the garage sale.

∼

It's June. We've downsized, sorted, packed. The move across town has happened, and we are now centered in a space that hasn't quite found itself or its identity, containing a rather amorphous mess of cartons, furniture, objects to be arranged. It's like being surrounded by seracs and erratics—a jumbled mountain-scape with barely enough oxygen for activity, let alone speed or precision. I feel as if I'm plodding, placing a foot here, and the next foot there, uncertain of the track through this rockfall of ice and stone. Fatigue almost paralyzes me. So this is base camp for the next ascent?

We will miss the house we had lived in for fifteen years; it has its own distinct southwestern ambience in this Northwest setting. Its own outlook across blue Lake Whatcom toward the Cascade foothills. Its personality that matched ours so well. We hope to sell it to someone who loves it as much as we have. The new, slimmed-down, efficient home that we've settled into will take time to feel familiar. Will our elderly belongings feel at home in it? Will we?

The house we left faced east towards the sunrise. The new house faces west, the direction of sunsets. I'm pondering the significance of this; a kind of melancholy attaches to this metaphor. And I'm doing some serious grieving for what I'm leaving behind.

Yet though the old house of my body isn't equipped, I must resolutely deal with the shock of this strenuous passage with its depleted oxygen and rarefied air.

Transition. This means that no matter how established or permanent our lives seem to be, we cannot settle in too comfortably in this new shelter, this bivouac on the mountainside. The upper reaches still wait for us to conquer them. We pray for courage and vigor for the next level.

# 18

## Experiencing Altitude

***In his book*** *Into Thin Air,* climber and author John Krakauer talks of "the staggering unreliability of the human mind at high altitude." Yet here we are. My human mind is still tolerably optimistic and reliable (I think), and I hope you are still climbing with me. I've invited you to join me in a season's worth of observing, pondering, regretting, questioning, accepting, all the while being grateful for this crazy, ongoing life of mine.

We still live within reach of Mt. Baker, nearly ten thousand feet tall. In our soggy Northwest weather, the mountain is often hidden behind mist and rain. We remind ourselves that it's there, whether we can see it or not. "The mountain's *out* today!" we sometimes call out to our neighbors.

Like God, who has sometimes, often, seemed invisible, like the sun once it has set, he has shown me the benefit of waiting, of being ready for change. I have glimpsed him in unexpected ways, and I have responded to this life I have been given with some misgivings but also real satisfaction, true hope.

I'm guessing about future possibilities, yet right now I am feeling gratitude for all that I've been given: "Bless the LORD, O my soul, and all that is within me, bless his holy name" (Psalm 103:1).

How long my life will continue on earth is still unknown. The future is a surprise package full of questions without answers. How my body and mind will respond to the inevitable deterioration remains to be seen.

Yet with Job, with Handel, I am learning to affirm, "For though worms destroy this body, yet in my flesh shall I see God" (Job 19:26, as rendered in *The Messiah*).

I can hear the composer's tune in my mind. Is this what we can look forward to? No limited horizons, no more hearing loss, bloody noses, partisan politics, obstacles, canceled flights, stink of sweat, time limits, cracked bones, methane gas, sagging, underarm hair, global warming, wrinkles, aches, flu, yellowing teeth, floods, adipose tissue, tumors, tsunamis, cataracts, betrayals, myopia, hurricanes, irregular heartbeats, diverticuli, road rage, dementia, spider veins, erectile dysfunction, purple bruises, developmental defects, moles, anxieties, thinning hair, shame, delusions of grandeur, scars, lost socks, bald heads, unfulfilled dreams, longings for truth, oil spills, contracts, credit cards, debts, highway gridlock, meanness of spirit, discords, deserts, doubts, blizzards, deadlines . . .

Dead-lines?

Age has its limitations. Old windows close. New ones open. Life is forever.

### Exit

*When you go,*
*will you go with a sizzle—*
*a spiteful spitting on a*
*hot plate,*
*a jig of steam?*
*With a crystal sigh on a beach*

*to leave a bubble?*
*Or will your trickle*
*run, thin, silver,*
*to the open ocean?*

*When you leave will you leave with a bang—*
*exploding like a*
*far star, kicking your*
*hot cinders in God's eye?*
*Or quietly, clinging*
*to your black match-stick corpus,*
*a slow blue shrinking*
*in the dark?*
*Or will your bud of burning*
*lift, bloom-bright,*
*to a wider light?*[1]

# Notes

### Chapter One: The View from Here

[1] Luci Shaw, "The Door, the Window," in *The Angles of Light* (Colorado Springs: Shaw/Waterbrook, 2000), p. 61.

[2] Sarah Payne Stuart, "Personal History: Pilgrim's Progress," *New Yorker,* July 30, 2012, p. 32.

### Chapter Two: Looking Ahead

[1] Emily Dickinson, "'Tis so much joy, 'tis so much joy . . . ," in *The Poems of Emily Dickinson,* ed. Thomas H. Johnson (Cambridge, MA: Belknap Press of Harvard University Press, 1951), pp. 131-32.

[2] Andrew Hudgins, "The Hereafter," in *American Rendering* (Boston: Houghton Mifflin Harcourt, 2006), p. 95.

### Chapter Three: Feasting on Distances

[1] Amy Frykholm, *Julian of Norwich: A Contemplative Biography* (Brewster, MA: Paraclete, 2010).

[2] Luci Shaw, "Weight Loss," in *Harvesting Fog* (Montrose, CO: Pinyon, 2010), p. 16.

### Chapter Four: Fit for the Climb?

[1] Luci Shaw, "Old Hand," in *Scape: New Poems* (Portland, OR: Wipf and Stock, 2013), p. 19.

[2] Shaw, "So It Is with the Spirit," in *Scape,* p. 15.

[3] Scott Cairns, "Ambiguity, Perplexity and Truth," *Huffington Post,* December 14, 2010.

### Chapter Five: Dangers Ahead?

[1] Tina Brown, editorial, *Daily Beast / Newsweek,* March 2011.

**Chapter Seven: Bivouacking**

[1] Luci Shaw, "Novel," in *Scape*, p. 34.

**Chapter Eight: Above the Tree Line**

[1] Stonewall Jackson, quoted by Atul Gawande, "Letting Go," *New Yorker*, August 30, 2010, p. 9.

[2] Jonathan Weiner, *Long for This World* (New York: Ecco/HarperCollins, 2011).

[3] John Wilson, review of Weiner's *Long for This World*, *Christianity Today*, October 2010, p. 61.

[4] Luci Shaw, "Engine," in *Scape*, p. 32.

**Chapter Ten: The View from the Slope**

[1] Luci Shaw, "Thunder and then," in *Scape*, p. 27.

**Chapter Eleven: Lightening the Load**

[1] Luci Shaw, "The Promise," in *Scape*, p. 21.

**Chapter Thirteen: Mountain Pilgrimage**

[1] Luci Shaw, "The separation," in *Polishing the Petoskey Stone* (Wheaton, IL: Harold Shaw, 1990), p. 232.

[2] "Onlookers," in ibid., p. 217.

**Chapter Fourteen: Incidents and Accidents**

[1] Luci Shaw, "Birthday," in *Scape*, p. 18.

**Chapter Sixteen: Companions on the Way**

[1] Ruth Pitter, quoted by Michael Ward in a review of Don King's *A Critical Biography of Ruth Pitter*, *Christianity and Literature* 58 (Spring 2009).

**Chapter Seventeen: The Grass Under Our Feet**

[1] Carolyn Forché, "Poetry of Witness," *Poetry*, May 2011.

[2] Rivka Galchen, "Dream Machine," *New Yorker*, May 2, 2011.

[3] Luci Shaw, "Flowerhead," in *Scape*, p. 23.

[4] Luci Shaw, "Credo," in *Scape*, p. 51.

**Chapter Eighteen: Experiencing Altitude**

[1] Luci Shaw, "Exit," in *Polishing the Petoskey Stone*, p. 83.